A KINGDOM BY THE SEA

An Exploration of Northumberland,
Durham and the North Riding
of Yorkshire

A KINGDOM BY THE SEA

An Exploration of Northumberland,
Durham and the North Riding
of Yorkshire

Betty James

HODDER AND STOUGHTON

Printed in Great Britain for Hodder and Stoughton Ltd.
St. Paul's House, Warwick Lane, London, E.C.4.
by Northumberland Press Ltd., Gateshead

For the London Geordies: Tommy Tomlinson,
Jack and Eileen . . . .
for Consie too, and with thanks to the
North-East Development Council for their
help and co-operation.

Contents

Illustrations

[1] Photo-Mayo Ltd.
[2] Turners (Photography) Ltd.
[3] Central Office of Information
[4] Northumberland County Council
[5] Philipson and Son Ltd.
[6] Industrial Pictorial Services
[7] North-East Development Council
[8] Bertram Unne
[9] Tindale's of Whitby
[10] Noel Habgood F.R.P.S.

Introduction

The North-East coast can be reached in 6 hours by road, 4 hours by rail, and 1 hour by air from London. It consists of 4,000 square miles incorporating Northumberland, County Durham, and the North Riding of Yorkshire. Every year, thousands of Southerners pass through it on their way to prang a grouse, land a salmon, clinch a deal in Scotland, entirely unaware that they have just missed a part of Britain so beautiful, so kindly, so gentle that it seems to contain within itself all that is now left of England.

Before being sent on a journalistic assignment to look at the Three Rivers—the Tyne, the Wear, and the Tees—I, too, may have thought of Hadrian's Wall as a rather pointless lump of old stone meandering across a moor, possibly somewhere near Edinburgh. Certainly I remember on arrival looking hopefully around for a sight of my first pit-heap. Now, however, I return to the North-East with delight, revisiting its lush green fields, bracing moors, and long golden beaches in order to escape for a while the stench of London—which stench has lately become almost tangible. Comparable to attempting to breathe through a dusty black boot-button stuffed up the nostril.

Though the population of the North-East is centred upon its three rivers, everybody also lives within easy reach of an unspoiled and greatly varied countryside, and of the sea. They have access to every possible form of sport including one or two of the more unconventional ones such as skin-diving—or ski-ing in the Cheviots for about 3 months in the winter. Due to the fact that the cost of living is lower than it is in the South (a

11

brand-new 3-bedroomed house might cost around £2,800), most of the nautically-inclined can also afford to buy a boat and join one of the twenty sailing clubs scattered along the coast and on one of the lakes.

Since it became bruited abroad that I was writing this book ('without even being *asked* to') I have been the recipient of desperate confidences from families being 'sent North' by their firms as if to the very last outpost of the British Empire. It appears that these families suffer from four outstanding anxieties apart from the one of housing with which I have already dealt. Before the regional descriptions which follow it might be well to deal with these anxieties.

Immigrants from London worry about (*a*) education, (*b*) making friends, (*c*) culture, and (*d*) most incredible of all— hospitals!

So far as education is concerned it would be well to (1) write to the appropriate local authority, (2) go and have a look at the Prissick Campus in Middlesbrough, a prototype of the equally beautiful, though less easily discoverable schools springing up all over the area, and (3) learn with surprise that the University of Durham is the oldest in England after Oxford and Cambridge.

Making friends in the North-East is almost embarrassingly easy so long as nobody comes-the-Londoner at them. But then coming-the-Londoner is equally unpopular from Peebles to Pontypridd. And jolly bad manners to boot.

I cannot help being amused by the culture bit: and for that matter neither can the North-Easterner. Ask the really eager-beaver Southern culture-vulture (without warning) what he attends in the way of mind-improvement when he's at home. Then watch while his face valiantly attempts not to crease in thought. "Grhooo!" he will state. "British Art Museum . . . er . . . Covent Pleasure Garden and . . . er . . . Maria Callas at the Festival Gallery . . . oh . . . yeah . . . Hilton Hotel . . . and . . . and that."

Ah, poor fellow, let us set his obviously so far unimproved mind at rest . . . Sandy Dunbar, secretary of the North-Eastern Association for the Arts, sees to it that each county gets its fair share of Sadler's Wells Opera, the Royal Ballet, Hamlet, Racine, 'Who's Afraid of Virginia Woolf?', Benjamin Britten, Munich

Philharmonic, pantomime, international film shows, jazz concerts, art exhibitions, the Georgian State Dance Company, and quite a few other things which are much too choosey ever to hit London at all. The North-East's own Chamber Orchestra—the Northern Sinfonia—presents, when it isn't in London or abroad, Moura Lympany, Adele Leigh, John Ogden, Geraint Evans, in every large town in the area. Their young conductor, Boris Brott, boasts a large teenage fan club, complete with airport welcomes: a fact of which not even the most rabid decrier of modern youth could disapprove.

The B.B.C. and Tyne-Tees Television gear their programmes to the interests of the area and also take in most of the better national programmes. And to those who imagine Tyne-Tees is two bits of wire held together by a paper-clip I would add that they have won 3 First and 1 Second major awards 4 years running for outstanding news films.

On the question of hospital services I can only say that, apart from the excellent facilities already there, there's a lot more room up North than there is down South for the building of even bigger and better hospitals. But one must always remember that the area is essentially healthy and less inclined towards drugs and pep-pills.

There's just one thing more about the area as a whole. The true Northerner suffers from a totally unnecessary inferiority complex, possibly enhanced by one or two particularly porcine gaffes perpetrated by politicians over the last few years. One out of every three of the inhabitants of the area will inevitably say to the visitor, "You thought we lived in caves and painted ourselves with woad, didn't you?"

On being assured that your ignorance had not actually reached limits so entirely unlikely he will ask you, "Whatever did you come here for then?" Thereafter, being a proper British gentleman, he will go limp with embarrassment at your praise of his beautiful and historic countryside. Digging his toe thoughtfully into the sand he will try to think of something nasty to say about it in deference to this mad lady who is trying to assure him how lucky he is to live where he does. And he will invariably come up with "Well now, Pet, our weather isn't very good, you see."

To him, and to the Southerner who persists in referring to it

13

as 'the Frozen North', I offer the following figures taken from Hartlepool, which is just about halfway through the area . . .

Daily Sunshine Average
    Hartlepool . . . 3·81 hours
    Greenwich . . . 3·77 hours

Annual Rainfall
    Hartlepool . . . 23·62 inches
    Greenwich . . . 24 inches

The North-East is robust, largely undiscovered, entirely enchanting. This book contains a Londoner's impressions of it, and I hope that in the course of the following pages the North-East may feel that I have done it as proud as it has—in much too short a time—done me.

BETTY JAMES

Part One

NORTHUMBERLAND

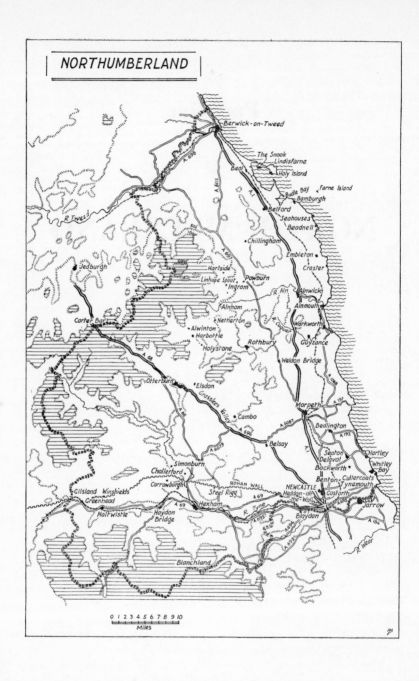

NORTHUMBERLAND

Berwick-on-Tweed

The Snook
Lindisfarne
Holy Island

Beal

Farne Island
Budle Bay
Bamburgh
Belford
Seahouses
Beadnell

R Tweed

Chillingham

Embleton
Craster

Jedburgh

Hartside
Linhope Spout
Ingram
Powburn

Alnham

R. Aln
Alnwick
Alnmouth

Netherton

Warkworth

Carter Bar

Alwinton
Harbottle
Holystone

Rothbury

R. Coquet

Guyzance

Weldon Bridge

Otterburn

Elsdon

Grasslees Valley

Cambo

Morpeth

Belsay

Bedlington

Simonburn

Chollerford
Carrowburgh

Steel Rigg

ROMAN WALL

Seaton
Delaval
Backworth

Hartley
Whitley Bay

Gilsland Winshields
Greenhead

Haltwhistle

Haydon
Bridge

Hexham

NEWCASTLE
Heddon-on-
the-Wall

R. Tyne

Benton Cullercoats
Gosforth

Tynemouth

Blaydon

Jarrow

R. Wear

Blanchland

0 1 2 3 4 5 6 7 8 9 10
Miles

Short History

Many otherwise quite intelligent people persist in thinking Northumberland to be in Scotland. They appear convinced that 'England' ends in a line running straight across from the Solway Firth.

This—naturally—upsets the Northumbrians.

Hadrian certainly built his Wall thus, but that was in A.D. 122 when he had excellent strategic reasons for so doing. The historical evidence of what happened to Britain both before and after A.D. 122 is still visible all over Northumberland in vast and fascinating profusion.

A comprehensive, yet easily-absorbed history of the area is impossible to discover. It is a history of bitter, cruel warfare and of the coming of Christianity. Certainly there is little room in this particular book for going into any great detail, and we shall mainly avoid the past and deal with the present. But to visit Northumberland with no idea whatsoever of its story is tantamount to visiting the supermarket without any money. You have to put everything back on the shelves and then start all over again.

The county, the fifth largest in England, consists of 2,016 square miles, the greatest length being 70 miles and the greatest breadth 47 miles. For those who have little time to consult their local library, rubbing up hurriedly on a rusty education, I append hereunder a very short outline. This will at least help the reader to appreciate the oustanding historical features in which the area is so rich. It will also enable him to understand what the rightly proud Northumbrian means when (in the understatement of all time) he flatly states that some of his fairly recent ancestors lived through 'claggy' times.

On the summits of the Cheviots in the Northumberland National Park are remains of ancient British encampments and burial grounds. These once consisted of a series of fortifications built round a central stronghold in which lived the Celts who, until their attention was turned on the advance of the Roman Legions from the south after 55 B.C., occupied themselves mainly in intermittent warfare against marauding tribes. That the barbarian Celts were determined and extremely courageous is evident from the enormous size of the forts and bastions built with magnificent engineering skill by the Romans to protect the northern outpost of their Empire against them. Of that Roman occupation much evidence remains in Northumberland and much more is still being discovered.

In the 5th century the Romans left Britain. In the 6th century Ida the Saxon landed and made Bamburgh the capital of his kingdom of Bernicia. He named it Din Guardi and built a castle there surrounded by a palisade. It was his grandson Ethelfrith who, in giving it to his wife Bebba, more nearly approached its present title by calling it Bebbanburgh.

The beginnings of Christianity arrived with Paulinus, a Roman missionary in the retinue of Queen Aedelberga when she married King Edwine in 617. Cadwallon, the pagan, killed Edwine and his successor in battle and was in turn slain by Oswald. From Oswald to Eanred most Saxon rulers in the area died violent deaths.

Meanwhile the monastic systems of Tynemouth, Hexham, Lindisfarne, Jarrow and Monkwearmouth were developing. These were the seats of any intellectual life Britain possessed. Gathering the tribes together into a loose political unity the Monasteries stood at their head for nearly a century, accustoming them to a national life of which the England of today is the heritage.

At the end of the 8th century the Danes appeared, burning and pillaging the monasteries, towns and villages. They behaved more as pirates than settlers, returning again and again to lay waste whatever had been salvaged.

Now began the great line of Northumbrian Earls. Under Danish overlords the Anglo-Saxons continued to be Earls of

Bamburgh and one of these—Osulph—contrived in A.D. 954 to throw off the Viking yoke by betraying the Scandinavian King Eric and bringing about his defeat and death in battle at Stainmore, in the Yorkshire Pennines. Osulph became Earl of Northumberland, probably the first to hold this title.

Thereafter one begins to sympathise with the Northumbrian in his 'claggy' times because at this point his troubles really started in earnest. Nchtred, son of Eadulf who succeeded Osulph, was assassinated at the court of Canute in 1016. Aldred, Nchtred's son, was also murdered and so was his half-brother (another Eadulf)—it is said by the next holder of the title, Siward. This was the Siward who battled against Macbeth to win back the Scottish crown for Malcolm. Siward also delivered himself of some famous last words on dying unexpectedly peacefully in 1055: "Shame on me that I did not die in battle, but am reserved to die with disgrace the death of a sick cow." Actually he was at the time lying in bed with his armour on, in singularly unbovine fashion, and clasping a battle-axe.

The earldom passed to Tostig who was killed by his brother King Harold at Stamford Bridge in 1066. William the Conqueror then gave the title to Copsi who was murdered after five weeks of government by Osulf, son of the Eadulf who preceded Siward, in the porch of Newburn Church. Then, as Symeon of Durham succinctly puts it: "Osulf himself perished in the autumn of the same year having transfixed himself with the spear of a robber, against whom he rushed with incautious precipitancy."

Gospatric then bought the earldom from William the Conqueror, but fell from favour and was succeeded by the Norman Robert de Comines, who was slain by the Northumbrians the day after his arrival in Durham. Gospatric then resumed the title only to be banished for treason in 1072. He was succeeded by Waltheof who lasted three years before being executed for conspiracy.

Walcher, Bishop of Durham, was appointed to the earldom only to be murdered at Gateshead in 1080. William then visited the North to quell his recalcitrant earls and burned it to the ground, sending a further army under his son Robert into Scotland against Malcolm. Malcolm in a counter-stroke destroyed what was left of Northumbria before he was killed at Alnwick in 1093. Robert de Mowbray, appointed in 1081 by

William I, now rebelled against William Rufus. By now, all over Northumberland, great fortresses and castles were rising on the hills in preparation for centuries of war against the Scots. In 1138 and 1174 the Scots overran Northumberland and perpetrated sickening atrocities. Even worse were the cruelties of King John, who in the course of an expedition to punish his Barons burned castles, towns and villages, killing and plundering without regard to age or sex. Wallace then led his wild Scots back through the countryside and Edward I retaliated. Robert Bruce repulsed Edward II at Bannockburn and subjected Northumberland to the unpleasant aftermath of yet another Scottish victory. No sooner had Edward III's Northern knights retrieved their honour at Neville's Cross than the Black Death destroyed one third of the remaining inhabitants. In 1388 the Scots defeated them once again at Otterburn.

In 1402 the Scots were again pushed back by the Earl of Northumberland and his son Henry Percy ('Harry Hotspur') but the Percys were also involved in a rising against Henry IV (see Shakespeare) and after Hotspur's death in battle at Shrewsbury the Earl was driven across the borders.

Another Scottish battle took place at Geteringe in 1415, followed by the Wars of the Roses with Northumberland battling on the side of the Lancastrians. In 1513, during the reign of Henry VIII, Lord Home ravaged the area but was defeated near Wooler. A few months later came the bloody battle of Flodden Field. In 1547 England again invaded Scotland. Peace followed in 1550, but raiding was resumed in 1557.

Meanwhile Henry VIII was bringing about the dissolution of the monasteries, much to the indignation of the Northern gentry. The Earls of Northumberland and Westmorland led an attempt to restore the faith in the reign of Queen Elizabeth in 1569 and one died on the scaffold, the other in exile. In 1588 and 1598 the Plague ravaged the North.

With the accession of James VI of Scotland to the throne of England the big Border battles ceased. In 1640 the Scots fighting against Charles I billeted themselves in Newcastle but in 1644 the Earl of Leven besieged the city for three weeks in February without success, and then moved Southwards. Leven (previously General Leslie) joined with Cromwell to defeat Prince Rupert at Marston Moor and then returned North again for a further siege of Newcastle, which lasted from August 12th to October 20th, when the city fell. The motto of the city of Newcastle: 'Fortiter Defendit Triumphans' is said to have been conferred by King Charles in recognition of this defence.

The Jacobite rebellion of 1715 in which the young and courageous Earl of Derwentwater proclaimed the Pretender at Rothbury, Warkworth, Morpeth and Hexham, came to a disastrous end and brought hopeless ruin to many famous Northumbrian families. The Earl was beheaded at Tower Hill in 1716 and his tragic death-mask is in the Black Gate Museum in Newcastle. His story is heartrendingly told in Anya Seton's 'Devil Water' and he is still remembered in the area by various songs and a Northumbrian pipe-tune, the famous 'Derwentwater's Lament'. An old lichened cross erected to his memory stands in the Tyne Valley near Langley Castle—now a girl's school.

If this short history has achieved its purpose it should at least have painted a more romantic picture of the area than the one generally visualised down South. I was in Northumberland a fortnight before I actually saw a pit-heap and that was only because I asked to see what a pit-heap looked like. Factory chimneys are relegated to development areas, just as they are on the outskirts of London. Certainly there are docks but—to me anyway—it is enormously exciting to stand next to a huge ship, floating, as it were, right in the middle of a city.

As to present history, Newcastle and Middlesbrough are now locked in a battle for supremacy just as fierce as the old Border battles, though less bloody at this point. The winner's perks are the sites chosen for new million-pound factories rather than a mere handful of sheep or cattle, but the determination is just as strong. Middlesbrough clearly intends to be Top.

However I must say that, on the whole, the Northumbrians behave somewhat as does the Londoner when confronted by the 'everything-we-have-is-bigger-and better' Texan line.

They just look faintly bored.

Public Transport

Since the last chapter was, of necessity, based somewhat heavily in the past I have thought it well to follow with these few notes, based, as they are, lightly in the present. All really dedicated sightseers avoid taking taxis if possible and in any case taxis in the North don't cruise around waiting to be hailed as they do in London. All provincial public transport has inherent quirks of one sort or another about which it is as well to be warned. Thus less time is wasted in finding out for oneself.

Nearly all North-Eastern buses are ultra-modern and very comfortable. The best ones are the bright yellow Newcastle buses which, says my favourite road-sweeper, "come at you like a bunch of bananas." But it's not coming *at* you you have to worry about. It's the fact that neither number nor destination is ever inscribed on the *back*. So you are required to scramble frustratingly to the front in order to discover which form of transport you've just missed.

All drivers and conductors are friendly and helpful. On the other hand all buses are driven in a series of frightful jerks. Useless therefore to rise from a top-deck seat one second before you intend to get off and then hope to ease yourself downstairs in time. Always get downstairs well before the bus, having braked wildly, decides to stop. Otherwise it will have shot off again with all four feet off the ground long before you've managed to gather either your wits or your balance.

Some Northern buses have seats for only one person in the front of the top deck. People used to London buses with their

22

invariable double seats are very apt, on reaching their destination, to slide along the bit which isn't there. This results in thudding to the floor, much to the surprise and consternation of the other passengers. North-Easterners have been trained from childhood to look right before leaving their seats and are therefore unable to comprehend why anybody should evince a sudden strange desire to lie flat on their backs in an omnibus.

Another unpleasant thing likely to happen to the novice is that he stands too near those new folding doors which are in use all over the North-East but as yet new to London. The driver has complete control of these doors and it is he who presses a little lever next to his wheel and waits for you to dismount. You stand there, still inside the bus, while the driver looks understandably puzzled. The reason you are still standing inside the bus is because your left foot has become inextricably mixed with the rubber base of the folding doors. You explain your predicament to the driver who obligingly puts the little lever into reverse, thereby elongating the toes on one of your feet beyond hope of repair.

Wise to this, you stand well back from the folding doors next time you are preparing to leave a bus, only to collect a smart punch on the nose from the edge of one of the folds, which blinds you for the rest of the afternoon.

Once one has learned to deal with them, however, North-Eastern buses are the best form of transport. Not only are the fares extremely cheap—especially in the North Riding—but also the Londoner can get quite a lot of amusement standing in a queue full of impatient Northerners muttering, "It's disgraceful. This bus is always at least 2 minutes late."

So far as trains are concerned, many of them are absolutely super. They take off like jet-planes, are spotlessly clean, extremely comfortable, and very punctual. My only criticism is that nearly all platforms suffer from the same coy desire to hide their identity. This means that wherever the stranger really meant to get off he invariably ends at the terminus in Newcastle. However, just opposite the station is a thriving all-night Wimpy Restaurant where Mr Weedy, the manager, does a succulent cheeseburger for 2/6d while his customers wait for the all-night bus to arrive and take them to wherever they intended to be in

23

the first instance. Sometimes, too, a hot-dog man cycles up and dispenses 1/3d worth of sausage-filled fresh roll.

In any case, missing a station at midnight up North any day of the week results in more civilised comforts than it does almost anywhere else.

Newcastle

Newcastle is the capital of the North-East, a city remarkable amid provincial monstrosities for the beauty of its architecture. It has the striking appearance of having been planned as a unit rather than of having been chucked up in a hurry as sudden necessity dictated and without looking where it was going. This is mainly due to three men; mid-19th-century architect John Dobson, builder Richard Grainger, and the Town Clerk of the time, John Clayton. Dobson was the son of a local innkeeper, Grainger started his career as a jobbing carpenter. In partnership they acted somewhat as did Napoleon in Paris, courageously demolishing anything likely to mar a clean and beautiful line. All things considered, however, Grainger and Dobson probably needed more courage than did Napoleon.

In any event, this is what probably helps to create the first impression absorbed by the newcomer—the impression that he is in a continental city. The lovely curve of Grey Street is an outstanding monument to the artistry of Grainger and Dobson, leading as it does up to the only readily recognisable Town Centre in England.

The second main impression jostles upon the first one. It is one of extreme cleanliness. That all Southerners expect thick dirt stems, I think, from the ubiquitous photograph of St Nicholas' Cathedral—sticking sootily up like a miner's pre-shower thumb—with which the Novocastrian persists in advertising his city. Possibly it is too late now for him to pick another, more modern image by which he may be readily recognised. Certainly one hopes he doesn't choose his new Civic

Centre—though I am more generously inclined than he is to think it may look better when it's finished.

The third impression is one of friendliness. "And what's this wee thing, Hinny? A typewriter is it!" marvels the porter at the station before disappearing without trace into a private labyrinth with your most precious possession.

From hand to anxious hand; from knowledgeable passenger to buffet attendant to Stationmaster, you, the Southerner, are finally directed to the entrance where your luggage reposes safely in the taxi upon which your porter is now leaning, explaining to the driver that that wee thing is a typewriter and that there is therefore a strong possibility that you are a writer. Cognisant of this strong possibility, your taxi-driver yields to a temptation to take you slightly out of your way because he wants to know what you think of the new Civic Centre. He spices his commentary with riveting, if probably apocryphal, snippets of chit-chat. "They built all the window-frames in bronze," he states, "and then found they couldn't open the windows to clean them. Lord Mayor can't see out to check the time."

"Horrible to live here," he surmises. "They're going to stick a carillion on top which'll play 'Blaydon Races' every quarter of an hour, night and day."

Everybody is interested, attentive, and polite. Your Southern accent does not deter the shop-assistant from apologising for not having what you want and then bothering to suggest another shop which probably stocks it. Your obvious anxiety to reach the lift in time does not deter the liftman from stopping halfway to the next floor and going smartly into reverse in order to come down again and pick you up. The waitress in the restaurant smiles at you and so does the loo-attendant. A request for street-directions results in strangers taking you almost to the door. And 'Whatever-did-you-come-here-for-then?' is the result of genuine concern rather than nosiness.

Sightseeing

It is a sad fact that most people are under the completely erroneous impression that they pay rates for a local library so that most other people may have free access to an unlimited number of time-wasting trashy novels and thrillers.

All Public Libraries happen also to be well-filled funds of local information; clearing houses for almost anything anybody might want to find out about. The first call when sightseeing anywhere in Britain should always be at the Central Library. The one in Newcastle, in New Bridge Street, houses one of the most efficient City Information Services in the country.

Among a mass of other literature they will produce lists of Places of Entertainment, Boarding Houses, Women's Organisations, Halls Available for Hire, Opening Hours for Principal Shops, and a comprehensive guide to Parking, on the back of which is a map indicating off-street car parks, number of bays, time limits, and charges. Newcastle does suffer from a morning and evening mini-jam, and although this is usually cleared by simple means of a 'duplicate' bus-service, it's as well to know where to leave the car while it's going on.

While you're at the library you should also pick up the invaluable free 'Guide to North-East England', published by the North-East Development Council, 20 Collingwood Street, Newcastle upon Tyne 1 (which will also be sent to you free if you write to them for it). This lists places of interest, with map references, art galleries and museums with opening and closing hours and entrance fees, hotels in North-East England, Youth Hostels, caravan and camp sites, places of entertainment, where to eat, cultural events, sports, sports clubs, special events for the year, suggested car tours, motoring organisations, late-night garages and petrol stations, car hire firms, consulates, European churches, and useful addresses of all kinds.

If you're thinking of staying long, ask also for a copy of the booklet 'Cultural Societies' which lists everything from numismatism to bell-ringing. One is a little downcast to discover that it doesn't include—as many London 'Town Guides' do—a Cactus and Succulent Society. But devotees of this particular form of devilment will undoubtedly discover that the Central Library is swiftly able to lay hands on the address of the local branch. If you're lucky they may also hand you a free copy of my favourite little thesis: 'How to say NO to a Doorstep Salesman'. This is a publication I feel nobody anywhere should be without—particularly if they're selling doorsteps.

Before leaving the library, check also on the bus and walking tours of Newcastle which have been arranged by the Assistant Librarian. These start from New Bridge Street every Wednesday during the summer at 7.15. Tickets for the bus tours are 2/6d. Walking tours are free and—in my opinion—much more fun.

Places of Interest (Historical and Cultural)

Henry II rebuilt the 'New Castle' of William Rufus (which Rufus, in turn, had built on the foundations of the 'Old Castle' of William the Conqueror's son—Robert Curthose) at a cost of £911 10s. 9d. which doesn't seem much until you remember that in Henry II's day an ox cost 3/- and a ram a mere 8d.

It should be remembered, however, that it was Henry III who added the BLACK GATE which stands at its base. Its name has nothing to do with its colour but originated from a 17th-century lessee, Patrick Black.

The Black Gate Museum is arranged in a series of cases illustrating the history of Newcastle. Particularly interesting is the Whittonstall Hoard of 1,150 Edward I and II pennies, the largest cache ever discovered. This obviously belonged to some cautious worthy who decided Shotley Bridge was safer than a bank and then forgot where Shotley was.

Look also at the Passing Bell, which was tolled during executions in the City Gaol until as late as 1925; the model of the Sandhill Pant erected by a kindly Corporation to dispense wine to the crowds on the coronation of George IV, and the Earl of Derwentwater's death-mask (see page 21).

Hard by the Black Gate is the KEEP, one of the finest in the country and all that now remains of Henry II's *Novum Castellum*. On entering one gains the impression of a historical building allowed to rely entirely upon its own powerful aura rather than on a costive conglomeration of pikes, halberds, suits of armour, stirrups, spurs and muskets, all arranged in highly unlikely formations and of no interest whatsoever to anybody bar an expert in ancient arms and armoury. The immediate reaction is a desire to climb to the topmost battlements where one may obtain a magnificent view of the splendid railway system covering seventeen acres, with two miles of platforms.

Those with imagination may like to visualise the scene below as it was before it was cleared in 1883 by the Society of Antiquaries. Until then it was a second-hand clothes market, particularly rich in navvies' brogues, their soles turned upward to prove the wealth of nails. Slumdwelling spectators lolled from broken casements in and around the Black Gate surveying the scene of squalor beneath. Dirty children and bedraggled hens picked their way through gutters running with filth beneath bunches of bright garments hanging on pegs above the customers.

Nowadays the second-hand clothes of Newcastle are sold from PADDY'S MARKET, Sandgate, on Saturday mornings. This market is run from a warehouse packed with rags and refrigerators in City Road, by the pavement of which stands a beautiful red Bedford van, complete with murmuration of musical horns and the largest accumulation of bonnet-badges extant. Nobody seems to know who 'Paddy' is but it is evident that Paddy has either travelled in many exotic lands or nicked an awful lot of badges.

From the Keep, descend by Dog Leap Stairs and The Side into Dean Street, then up past Bart Snowball the Saddlers' into the graceful curve of Grey Street towards the Theatre Royal. On Saturdays and general holidays one may obtain a wonderful view by paying 6d and climbing up inside the GREY MONUMENT but I feel it imperative to point out that anybody suffering even minimally from vertigo should avoid this absolutely petrifying experience.

Earl Grey of Howick is indissolubly connected with the Reform Bill which, for anybody finding it difficult to connect anything whatsoever with the Reform Bill, means that he did a great deal to ensure that almost *any*body could become an M.P. Present experience proves beyond doubt that Earl Grey of Howick certainly succeeded.

The MUSEUM OF ANTIQUARIES in the University buildings is best left until one has had one's preliminary view of the Roman Wall. The LAING ART GALLERY at the back of the Central Library see page 27) is interesting in that it owns a lovely Epstein head, a Henry Moore, and was the place chosen for the first British exhibition of Indian Art, which then by-passed London and went to Ghent. Do not miss the strange self-portrait of Sir William Orpen, who appears to have executed his own very personal masterpiece while clad in a spotless terry-towelling bathrobe, minuscule spectacles, and a huckaback headpiece firmly anchored to his brow with a wide blue satin ribbon.

Not far from here is the PLUMMER TOWER, which once formed part of the Town Wall and was last used in the defence of the city when the Mayor held out against the Earl of Leven in 1644 (see page 20). It was refronted by the Freemasons in 1750 and at one time used as a private house. It is now an archive exhibition centre, and when I was there last the theme was Public Health in Newcastle. "Amputation-knife" ran the horrid captions to the dentistry section. "Saw of stout construction. Pliers with sharp cutting-edge, and triangular needles. Mouth-gag with thumb-screws. Elevator for the extraction of roots. Forceps: Crow-Bill type."

The MUSEUM OF SCIENCE AND ENGINEERING, beautifully located by the boating lake in Exhibition Park, adjoining the Town Moor, is the city's pride and joy. Useless to state that, being female, you don't really understand Science and Engineering, since this is but to court total social obloquy.

The museum consists of over eight thousand exhibits devoted to the history and development of the engineering, shipbuilding, mining, electrical, chemical, and transport industries, of which the area owns so important a share. George Stephenson, who was born in 1781 at Wylam, near Newcastle, is quite naturally a famous local hero and his *Killingworth Billy* stands here on the original Stockton-to-Darlington lines of which we shall say more later. His son built the High Level Bridge over the Tyne, the crossing of which on the way from Gateshead means to every Novocastrian that he's home.

In a special hall is the graceful *s.s. Turbinia*. Though the principal of steam turbines was actually invented by Hero, an Alexandrian, in 130 B.C., it was Sir Charles Parsons who converted them to electrical power generation, from which descends the present-day activities of C. A. Parsons & Co. of Newcastle. He took *Turbinia*, built in 1894, to Spithead in 1897 where it shot nippily ahead of the ponderously lumbering Naval Review, much to the discomfiture of the Admiralty, who had refused to take any interest in it until that moment.

The Town Moor beside which the Museum stands covers 927 acres and was for a long time the subject of dispute between the Freemen of the City and the magistrates. An Act of 1773 vested ownership in the Corporation but promised the right of two milch cows to graze thereon to each resident Freeman or his widow forever. But by a curious decision the Freemen hold the grass, not while it is growing but only when it is being cropped or is actually cut. The greatest revenue is obtained from the Hoppings Fair, which is the largest in the world, covers 25 acres, and takes place once a year in the last full week of June. Estimates put the attendance at the Hoppings at 1 million each year.

New plans for the Moor to be turned into the most modern playground in Britain include restaurants, woods, nature reserves, botanical gardens, golf courses, ski and toboggan runs, and a go-kart track. There will however still be room left for over 1,000 Freemen to graze 386 cows—the Freemen with these more fortunate cows to be drawn annually by lot. As recently as 1948 the Council were trying to promote a Parliamentary Bill giving them complete control of the Moor. But the title of Freeman has passed from father to son for more than 1,400 years since Saxon times and even the go-kart track—the newest-fangled idea of the lot—wasn't going to displace them and their milch-cows whatever some grasping Alderman or other might choose to have hoped.

Since the Town Moor is always followed by 'and Jesmond Dene' by all Novocastrians describing their home town this seems a good place in which to mention this lovely little valley. It is attached to Armstrong Park and was given by Lord Armstrong to the city. No child can really have had a proper old-fashioned childhood who has not played cowboys-and-Indians, fished, found caves, explored, climbed trees, and almost drowned in the miniature Niagara falling over the rocks into the stream. Its steep sides are covered in season with heather, rhododendron, primrose, and cowslip. I once walked there at dawn on a Sunday to wake up the birds and discovered, on the way back, a shop in Jesmond open at 6.30 a.m. where the only grocery it was too early to buy was liquor from the wine department.

Talking of birds, the HANCOCK MUSEUM not far from the University is one of the finest Natural History museums in the country, wherein may be found many of the examples used by Thomas Bewick for his famous 'History of British Birds'. There are also specimens of fish, insects both British and foreign, reptiles, fossils, and shells.

To return to historical sites, ST NICHOLAS' CATHEDRAL CHURCH dates back to the middle of the 14th century but only became a cathedral in 1882. A lantern to guide travellers home has for centuries gleamed from the 'Scots Crown'.

On the square outside is a statue of Queen Victoria, fashioned by Alfred Gilbert. She squats in the shade of a tortuous metal canopy, and due to her expression of deep anxiety it is considered by experts to be one of the least hypocritical of public statues in the country. It is possible however that her mien of suppressed rage may be due to the fact that she is wondering how to get the hell out of Newcastle while preserving at the same time her dignity. Her canopy is indeed highly decorative but Mr Gilbert seems to have failed to realise that the poor lady cannot possibly be expected to rise to her feet without seriously dislodging her crown and that her only means of escape is therefore that of slithering grumpily downwards on the back of her spine, thereby retaining her headpiece if not her composure.

The spire of the Roman Catholic Cathedral of ST MARY'S was designed in 1834 by the Mr Hansom who also designed the cabs. And ALL SAINTS' down by the quayside is one of the very few oval churches left in the country.

The quayside is approached by a series of little paths and winding steps called 'chares' with fabulous views of the riverside at every turn—not black as expected, but rose-pink, grey, blue and green. Down here is also the 17th-century Surtees House standing in what was once a very fashionable quarter. There is a plaque under the casement from which Bessie Surtees eloped precariously down a ladder in 1772 into the arms of John Scott, the future Lord Eldon, Lord Chancellor of England.

Spare a thought also for poor John Wesley who, 30 years earlier, had stood on the GUILDHALL steps and given voice to the Hundredth Psalm. This appears to have caused some local disrelish since he recorded in his Journal that 'three or four people came to see what was the matter.' Once they discovered that what was the matter was John Wesley they were joined by a whole lot of other people who attempted somewhat forcibly to dissuade him immediately. He was finally rescued by a fishwife —name of Mrs Bailes—who flung her biceps around his chest, thereby very sensibly knocking the breath out of the Hundredth Psalm, and called him a 'canny man'.

The Corinthian-style
portico of the Theatre Royal,
Newcastle upon Tyne

The Sunday morning
market on the Quayside
at Newcastle

A stretch of Hadrian's Wall

Bamburgh Castle

There is an interesting reference to Wesley's wife in ST ANDREW'S (which vies gamely with ST JOHN'S for the honour of being the oldest church in Newcastle) in the churchyard. In fact Wesley avoided matrimony until he was 47 and then rather foolishly allowed himself to be hooked by a wealthy widow with four children, who nagged him intolerably and occasionally dragged him around the floor by his hair. Five years before she died she left him, which is not mentioned on the tomb of the Smiths who proudly announce thereon: ". . . the above Jane Smith was the daughter of Anthony & Mary Vazelle. The latter, when a widow, married the Rev. John Wesley . . . and was buried in Camberwell Churchyard on October 12, 1781." Quite an intricate exercise in early public relations for the Smith family this.

Culturally the THEATRE ROYAL presents the London West End shows considered worthy of the highly discriminating North-Eastern audiences. But it is the PEOPLE'S THEATRE ARTS GROUP, the largest organisation of its kind in the world, which is the more famous. It began almost accidentally in 1911 with a handful of people presenting plays in a small room in Leazes Park Road. One of the founders, the late Norman Veitch, who wrote a book on the subject, said at the time, "If we're going to murder plays, let's murder the best" and so they started with Shaw, including 'The Shewing-up of Blanco Posnet', which had just been banned by the Lord Chamberlain for public performance. In 1915 they moved to more spacious premises, and in 1924 they became the second theatre (and the first amateur one) to produce his 'Back to Methuselah'.

Their aim was to present to Tyneside audiences plays of interest and quality and this policy has served as a guide-line ever since. The list of productions has been described by Ursula Jeans as the finest collection of plays a theatre has ever produced.

In 1929 they moved to Rye Hill where they remained for 32 years and 503 productions, surviving World War II with difficulty. At the end of the war the Tyneside Film Society amalgamated with the People's Theatre, followed shortly afterwards by the Tyneside Music Society. Small art exhibitions were mounted for the benefit of theatre audiences and for all these productions the same basic criteria were applied—the requirement was for quality and interest, from all periods and from all over the world. By this time the People's was presenting its activities in 6 different halls in Newcastle.

After a long and tedious search for a home of their own, the People's—by now presenting pieces by 'unknowns' such as Harold Pinter and John Whiting—finally bought a large modern cinema. The cost was £27,500 and totally exhausted their accumulated savings. An appeal was launched to convert the cinema to an Arts' Theatre. Such is the enthusiasm of the North for its own phenomenal successes in cultural activity that money started to come in—from a lady who sent a postal order because she was thinking of the People's when the laundry called with a refund, to a £17,000 grant from the Calouste Gulbenkian Foundation. From regular matchboxes full of halfpennies from a devoted audience member, to over £30,000 from local authorities and substantial sums from industry.

The People's have now achieved their first objective—an Arts' Centre for Tyneside that houses plays, films, concerts, ballet, opera, art exhibitions and a thriving Youth Theatre. The total cost was over £180,000, but more than 80 per cent of this had been raised before the appeal was 5 years old. And it has all been done by amateurs.

Volunteers to man the box-office, electricians to cope with the stage-lighting, tailors to make the costumes, seamstresses, hairdressers . . . all these are welcome to join—free—for 6 months on a prospective basis. Final acceptance to the rota of full members depends on proven willingness to apply oneself to the job.

The equipment is the most modern available, membership cuts across all sections of the community. Productions are rehearsed for 6 weeks and the House is usually Full. Anybody aspiring to act has to remember that there are no stars . . . only players, and that at the end of the play the curtain falls but once. It does not rise again however much the audience may applaud, because this is a community effort in which the props-man and the Green Room bar-attendant are just as important as the actors.

Before we leave the cultural for the mundane there are just three more places worthy of particular mention. Newcastle's well known LITERARY & PHILOSOPHICAL SOCIETY, the 'Lit & Phil' founded in 1793 by a couple of reverend gentlemen and a few townspeople interested in literary and scientific matters. It is built on the site of the town house of the Earls of Westmorland. Robert Stephenson left the Society £10,000 in his Will. It now contains over 100,000 books and 2,000 are added annually. There are also 3,000 musical scores and a record library with a choice of 2,500 discs, 450 of which are long-playing. It also contains a study-room and a lecture theatre with 500 seats which was donated by Lord Armstrong. The annual subscription is 4 guineas.

The only place in Britain used as a permanent home for modern poetry is also in Newcastle, in the MORDEN TOWER set in the West Wall of the city. This was inaugurated by Tom Pickard, a shaggy young poet who has been considerably encouraged by the North-Eastern Association for the Arts, who give him grants to help him carry on.

And last, the STONE GALLERY just opposite the Civic Centre, an admittedly commercial enterprise, but a very interesting one. Mr and Mrs 'Mick' Marshall, the owners of the gallery, once ran an art shop in the city, from which vantage point it did not take them long to realise that Newcastle leads all other provincial cities in its appreciation of the visual arts. "Up here," Mick told me, "if they like it, they buy it. And what they like is highly *avant-garde*." Nowadays the Marshalls sell paintings priced from 5 to 5,000 guineas, mainly by-passing London, to people entirely unconcerned with status symbols. The Stone Gallery has also become a Saturday morning meeting place for actors playing in the city theatres, musicians, journalists, and anybody else who feels like arguing until 5.30 on Sunday morning about matters entirely esoteric.

Eating and Drinking

Mr John Dean, Resident Manager of the ROYAL TURK'S HEAD HOTEL in Grey Street, is also chairman of the Northern Division of the British Hotels and Restaurants Association. He agrees that restaurants in Newcastle have improved beyond recognition over the last 5 years. "A directorate and executive class has arrived from London to live here," he said, "and they want to eat out. Eight years ago Newcastle was dead from the crop up. A chap taking a girl out spent very little on food and nothing on drink. It's very different now, but food and service still have to be very good. The Northerner expects value for money—he always will. And nobody lasts long who doesn't give it to him."

The Royal Turk's is rich and well-sprung. It retains the old-world atmosphere so lacking in the modern somebody-is-waiting-to-move-in (so will you please pay your bill and get out) hotel. The restaurant is excellent and I must particularly recommend the Red Rover Bar, which is entered via a replica of the Red Rover coach which once ran from the door of the Turk's Head to Edinburgh. At lunchtime there is a well-stocked buffet and every evening a pint of beer is drawn to the memory of some guardsman of doubtful fame. It is left on a shelf until the last customer has departed and the potman downs it. The hotel itself is used by all the more famous actors and actresses playing at the Theatre Royal opposite.

If it's tulle, white tie, and tempo top twenty you want then the ROYAL STATION HOTEL will provide it for you on Saturday evenings from the end of October to the beginning of April. Here I would also recommend the Cocktail Bar any day of the week, where Emmanuele Biagio makes his rye-and-dry with orange bitters and fresh orange slices and knows more than he care to divulge about the so-called Travelling Expenses of the hangers-on to the rich shipping landowners hereabouts. Everybody in this bar looks exactly like a Tyne-Tees film director having a quiet think—but Biagio can tell a rivet-pusher from a South Welsh laminate-salesman before you've even swallowed your first stuffed olive.

The Rank Organisation has recently opened its FIVE BRIDGES HOTEL in Gateshead, where the locale is not as romantic as the name of the hostelry, and wherein many North-Easterners sit and wonder if the décor of wheels and cogs is supposed to be an insult to their present or a paean to their past. But the newest and most modern luxury spot is the GOSFORTH PARK HOTEL, beautifully situated slap on the race-track and next to the famous NORTHUMBERLAND COUNTY GOLF COURSE. This hotel opened in October 1966 and from what one hears it should turn out to be the one really super place Newcastle has lacked up to now.

For just eating and drinking there are myriad restaurants catering from fish-and-chips to Egg Fu-Yong (also frequently with chips, since the Novocastrian, to the despair of many an earnest maître d'hôtel, refuses to forego them).

My special favourite is JIM'S INN in North Street, which specialises in steaks and has its 'Steak News' attached to the middle of an enormous 4-page menu. In décor it resembles a wildly expensive City of London chop-house but you can eat there for £1 a head so long as you are able to resist heaped platefuls from the tantalising refrigerated display cabinets.

The Cocktail Bar is comfortably upholstered to cushion the shuddering elbow—as are most of the really up-to-date bars all over the North-East—and offers a choice of fully 5 draught beers; which fact seems to drive most of the London Geordies I know to the verge of delirium.

TILLEY'S in Northumberland Road is a good spot in which to view the titled and the County taking coffee or sherry with their hats on in the Lounge on Saturday mornings. It is also the kiss of death for the Northern *nouveaux riches* since there's nothing more vulgar than sporting a diamond-covered rib-case when sitting right next to a Duchess who hasn't had time to change after milking the cows.

Tilley's also has an excellent restaurant upstairs where the Chicken à la King (15/-) is particularly to be recommended and where Mr Redmond, the Manager, will lend you his own glasses if you've forgotten yours and can't read the menu.

The RISTORANTE ROMA at 22 Collingwood Street is a relatively new Italian restaurant run by Mario Neri and Pascale Fulgenzi. They were waiters in the city until they realised that Newcastle husbands had realised that nibbling the wife's ear over a bit of candlelight now and then wasn't going to put any particularly deviationist ideas into her mind. The *Lasagna* here is piping hot (not all that easy unless the cook is concentrating) and the *Costolette di Vitello Lollobrigida* costs 15/6. People not wishing to nibble their wife's ears may sit at a communal middle table listening to Italian music and wondering sadly why no North-Eastern woman will ever sit alone at a communal table and be matey.

The best fish restaurant is FRED LINDSAY'S opposite the Central Station. One is a mite surprised to find the place entirely decorated in tartan but possibly this is in deference to the owner and not his wares. Right next to the restaurant is a counter from which are sold the enormous mussels and large succulent scampi native to these coasts. Lobsters are cheap but it's doubtful that you may be able to take one home and *Newburg* it as expertly as Fred does it in the restaurant.

Then there's the ELDON GRILL; but this is very masculine and mere women may not even sit on the bar-stools, much less stand libidinously around waiting for somebody to pass them a small port. Actually, unattached women standing around in *any* drinking-place up North are apt to attract a great deal of unwelcome interest of one type or another. The North is very much a man's world, but most sensible women are apt to discover they *like* being treated like women again, once they get used to it.

Most sensible women also lunch at Fenwick's. Which brings us to shopping.

Shopping

On being asked what fashions are like up North I have always replied—frequently much to the affronted rage of the Londoner—that FENWICK'S in Newcastle refer to Fenwick's in London as 'our Bond Street branch'. Fenwick's in Newcastle is twice the size of Fenwick's in Bond Street and was opened 10 years earlier, in 1882. Apart from exactly the same advanced styles, beauty preparations, and accessories (which are easier to obtain in different sizes and colours because they are actually stored on the premises) they also sell food and household goods and are appreciably less expensive because the overheads are much more reasonable.

Shopping and general embellishment of the person is much cheaper in the North-East anyway. The top hairdressers charge 12/6d for a 25/- London-type shampoo-and-set. One suit, a pair of slacks and a fur-lined jacket were cleaned for me by a well-known London-based cleaner for 15/11d. An ex-London interior decorator, Jack Hough, told me that R. J. MORPETH, for whom he now works, charge approximately 20 per cent less than he used to have to charge down south for laying a carpet, mainly because "the workmen are quicker and more efficient".

Naturally MARKS AND SPENCERS and all the other inescapable chain stores are well represented. On the other hand BINNS and BAINBRIDGES proudly and efficiently uphold local tradition.

The shoe shops all appear to stock shoes much more exciting than those in the West End of London but this may be because it is easier to cross the road to look in another window without risk of becoming irreparably bent in transit. TIMPSON'S the local chain store, are especially helpful and pack all their shoes into super little takeaway striped plastic shoe-bags.

On Saturdays, husbands and boy-friends join wives and sweethearts for the sake of a bit of masculine advice with the gear. They walk arm in arm past placards announcing, with typical Northumbrian caution, 'The Scott Umbrella Covers The North!' or 'Don't Forget Your Holiday Rainwear!' Taking no notice of all these unnecessarily depressive notices they plunge happily into piles of bikinis, surfacing occasionally to mutter, "F'r pity's sake mak oop y'r *mind* Gwen."

"Well," Gwen opines, "I'm not paying 12/11d for *this* clarty bit of polka-dot anyway."

To my own particular delight, many street corners are decorated with terribly clean golden ladies standing on tiptoe, stark naked. These belong to the NORTHERN GOLDSMITHS ('Holders of the Watch Record at Kew'), who have stationed one of them on the corner of Clayton Street and Westgate Road where she raises her graceful arms in permanent dismay at the sight of TOP RANK DANCING on the opposite corner.

Markets are: BIGG MARKET with its small trestles and stalls standing brightly where once was the barley exchange. GRAINGER STREET COVERED MARKET which opens in a burst of noise and colour around 6.00 every morning, excluding Sunday, and sells everything from toffee apples, through roses, to crown of lamb. And the QUAYSIDE SUNDAY MARKET which starts around 9.30 a.m. and of which Petticoat Lane is a mere pale copy.

No sightseer should miss the Sunday market, and especially the first sight of it from the top of one of the 'chares', spilling gaily along the quayside beside the enormous seagoing vessels, small tugs, and silent warehouses.

Most local grocers are also open on Sunday mornings. NICHOL'S in Brentwood Avenue, Jesmond, general dealers and off-licence, is open from 7.45 a.m. to 9.0 p.m. six days a week and 9.0 a.m. to 2.0 p.m. and 7.0 p.m. to 9.0 p.m. on Sundays.

After Sunday shopping many Novocastrians take a river trip for 5/- to the Harbour and back. These, and day outings to

Ryton Willows along the Tyne, take place at certain times of the year only, so it's safest to get a Sailing List from Mid-Tyne Ferries at Hebburn.

How It's Done

For those who like to see how things are made, the Central Library has produced a list of places to be visited free. Most of these places dish out cups of tea, biscuits and samples for nothing, too—though they don't often do it twice for the same person.

If you saw, for example, the care taken by PROCTER & GAMBLE—one of whose manufacturing plants is right in the middle of Newcastle—to ensure that your 'Daz' and 'Fairy Soap' are of exactly the right weight and quality you'd realise that the consistent giving away of free samples on site would be even dicier for the housewife's purse than are those grotty plastic tulips nobody in their right minds could ever look at without wincing.

If ever I am famous and rich enough to have *everything*, and some downtrodden journalist trying to make up a Christmas column rings up to ask me and Mrs Nubar Gulbenkian what we would most like as a present—then I'm going to say the one thing I most desire is a toothpaste-packing machine like the one at Procter & Gamble. This talented small contraption hums— very softly—"Titoothay—titoothay . . ." as it turns the tubes to the correct angle by means of an electronic eye, fills them soothingly (from the *bottom*—which is an education in itself), twists on the caps, and crimps up the nether-ends beyond hope of ham-fisted squeezure by hungover male persons in the morning.

You can, of course, watch cigarettes being rolled, ships being repaired, newspapers tumbling off the press. But the other thing which fascinated me, personally, was California Syrup of Figs which is produced by PHILLIPS, SCOTT & TURNER in Gosforth. There were various indignities one had to endure in my young days and one of them was definitely California Syrup of Figs. I was brought up on the Belgian principle that if a child is tetchy it's bunged up somewhere. Since no Belgian child was ever permitted to be anything worse that tetchy I have no doubt that the Belgians were probably entirely correct. So I took my tablespoonful of Syrup of Figs, allowed my governess to shove me into my scratchy starched pinny after all, and was jolly glad when I grew up.

Apart from the fact that Phillips, Scott & Turner also invented 'Shift' which I consider to be the housewives' all-time boon, they also manufacture Andrews Liver Salts. This started in 1894 in Newcastle's Gallowgate when a Mr Scott joined with a Mr Turner to compound a new effervescent health salt which they called after the church of St Andrews opposite Mr Scott's grocery and drysaltery warehouse. Nowadays it takes 45 minutes for the salts to tumble into a tin which started across the way as a piece of unprinted sheet-metal, to be sealed at the bottom, checked, firmly lidded, stamped with the date, re-checked, and sent at 150 tins a minute, printed in 30 different languages, at 8,000 lbs. an hour, straight into the carton. As it reaches the carton stage, each little tin hops with happiness. *Whoops* it goes. Some un-imaginative clot tried to tell me that it does that in order to get into the carton the right way up. What nonsense that is! If they want tins in cartons the right way up all they need to do is to move the cartons. I am perfectly certain that all those little tins were merely effervescently aware that they were off to spread inner cleanliness all over Europe.

Night Life
There are, as we go to press, 9 luxurious night clubs in New-castle. There are also several hundred pubs. The *vin du pays* is Newcastle Brown Ale, which Scottish & Newcastle Breweries turn out at the rate of 1,500 bottles per minute and which should be approached with the utmost caution. Southerners under the mistaken impression that Newcastle Brown Ale bears any resem-blance to any other brown ale are likely to land screaming in Ward 11 of the local hospital, which ward is said to be reserved especially for just such contingencies. It is also as well to remem-ber that when a North-Easterner says 'a pint of Scotch' he means Scotch Ale and not whisky.

I find it difficult to recommend one pub rather than another, since drinking in Newcastle is more localised than it is in London and the inhabitants are more likely to gravitate to the nearest pub with good dominoes than they are to worry much about the décor or the other drinkers.

Strangers are more welcome a little out of town. For instance at the tiny, cosy BEE HIVE in Hartley, which has been in the family of Vic and Joyce Shipley for 100 years. There is no bar as the Londoner understands a bar. Just two rooms—the Gun Room and the Harness Room. In between these stand Vic and Joyce behind their little counter, dispensing smiles, chit-chat, liquor, charm, and potato-crisps.

At the other end of the scale is what must be the most enormous Free House in Britain—the NEWTON PARK HOTEL at Benton. Obviously expense was no object when the cocktail bar was entirely papered in genuine goatskin. The Newton Park appears to have unlimited bars, halls, restaurants, and ballrooms, though I have to admit that I stayed closest to the unlimited free snacks in the well-upholstered goatskin cocktail bar.

For a surprisingly smooth little drinking club try the PILGRIM'S in Hutton Terrace at the back of Jesmond. Very smart indeed, this, with a Grill Room and appropriately under-lit cocktail bar. All sorts of unlikely characters come in with carnations in their buttonholes and expansive desires to buy drinks for everybody. The Manager is Ralph Wilkinson. It is open from 11.30 a.m. until 1.0 p.m. and 3.0 until 11.30 and—if you like little drinking clubs—I can't think of one in London to better it.

For the younger generation there is the Folksong & Ballad which takes place every Thursday at 7.30 p.m. at the BRIDGE HOTEL, Castle Garth. These sessions are quite astonishing. The strong and extremely well-set-up young men and girls of Newcastle enjoy singing their traditional songs—'The Keel Row', 'Cushy Butterfield', and 'When Jones's Ale Was New'. On alternate Tuesdays there is a Ceilidh Night with hornpipes and Morris dancing. But the rest of the time there is absolute silence from the audience, apart from a clacking of 'bones', as a ballad singer—who has probably paid his own fare all the way from Keswick—sings unaccompanied, or Johnnie Handel plays his fiddle.

Folksong & Ballad is neither a club nor a society. It is an organisation concerned exclusively with promoting a wider appreciation and deeper understanding of traditional folksong, balladry, and instrumental folk music of the British Isles, and especially that of Northumbria. It also seeks to encourage the contemporary work within this culture. Entrance fee is 2/6d

42

but the musicians aren't paid. They do it because they like it.

At BALMBRA'S—once the venue for the coaches going to Blaydon Races—old-time music hall is put on every evening, excluding Sundays, at 7.45 p.m. and 9.15. The stage is tiny and set at the end of a long room furnished with Victoriana most collectors would give a good deal to possess. Outside Olive Herdman's Blaydon Bar, Jack the doorman, and Stephen the waiter gaze enchanted at the week's programme announcing such gems as 'The Man with Educated Feet'. Inside, Dick Irwin gets ready to sing 'Daisy' or 'If You Knew Susie' to banquettes-full of happy ladies out on a spree. There are many clapping songs, some stamping songs, somebody is twenty-one today. The atmosphere is contagious. You forget how damn silly you probably look belting out ". . . you're my heart's desire. I love you, NELLie . . ." The show ends with Cindy, Sybil, and Margaret executing a spirited Can-Can amid a chorus of whistles from a party of sporty gents who have travelled from London to attend a course at the Ministry of Social Security, whose headquarters are in Newcastle. Balmbra's is owned by Charringtons and is situated not far from Bigg Market.

Most night-clubs are owned by the Bailey Organisation, which was started by two smart local boys who cottoned on to this latest type of North-Eastern pastime and now build entire Odeon-type erections to house them. But 'night-club' up North doesn't mean a tatty stuffed poodle and an empty box of chocolates for a tired hostess. It means a friendly bar where one may buy beer; a dance floor and cabaret starring P. J. Proby, Adam Faith, Kathy Kirby, Billy Daniels, Diana Dors, or Val Doonican. And nowadays it also means a gambling room or two. Membership is about a guinea, there is no entrance fee but there is sometimes a cover charge of around 5/- for special cabarets. Meals can be as little as 7/6d, and it is quite in order to buy a glass of beer and to stand there watching the cabaret without attracting the glittering gaze of the management.

Apart from my own favourite night-club, which I have described in another chapter, they mostly remind me of Mecca Dance Hall crossed rather hurriedly with Lyons Corner House. But like the capital city of the North-East—Newcastle itself— they're much more entertaining than you think they'll be before you get there.

Tynemouth

Nobody who is anybody ever actually *lives* in Newcastle. The 'in' thing is to live out, either in the country or on the coast, which is within 15 miles of commuting without strap-hanging. To the newcomer WHITLEY BAY, 10 miles from the city centre, may seem at first sight to be the most attractive seaside resort in the area, beset as it is with rock gardens, fun fairs, and that. It is only right, however, to warn him that Whitley Bay is also a favourite summer-hol spot for Glaswegians in search of wha' hae.

At the other end of the scale is CULLERCOATS, a small fishing village where once Polly Donkin (so they say) sold fresh crab, lobsters, winkles, and shrimps, from a trestle table outside her fisherman's cottage. The cottages there have lately been demolished and what Polly Donkin must have said about that I shudder to think. But, when the wind's in the right quarter, fresh seafood is still available at prices guaranteed to give Madame Prunier apoplexy.

Most of the really knowledgeable people, plus a large handful of London expatriates, live in TYNEMOUTH, a bracing spot with good sands and swimming. Tynemouth was once a fashionable 18th-century watering place, which accounts for the somewhat raffish air of the stately terraced houses along the front, now loosely converted into flats.

An enormous statue of Admiral Collingwood—one of Northumberland's most famous sons—gazes out over the treacherous Black Middens. It is not generally known that it was he who led the British Fleet into action at Trafalgar, keeping the enemy at bay for an hour before the rest of the ships sailed within gunshot.

On the jutting sandstone headlands are the ruins of the Priory of St Mary and St Oswyn. This headland has been fortified since earliest recorded times and monastic buildings have also stood there for over 1,300 years. Here Earl Tostig, brother of Harold of Hastings, had a fortress—and in 1100 the monastery became a sort of Reform School for unmanageable monks.

Not long ago an American film director was being shown the sights of Tynemouth by a prideful local inhabitant. As they reached the ruins of the Priory surrounding its carefully restored little chapel the American exclaimed, "My, my! This sure will look good when it's finished!"

"Mawthering fule!" muttered the prideful local inhabitant as he relayed this incident over a 'pint of Scotch' at the Rock of Gibraltar.

THE ROCK OF GIBRALTAR, a Charrington pub on the edge of the sea, is managed by Jim and Maureen Frazer and a very beady parrot. The parrot has been there since 1921, which is before Jim and Maureen were born. Until they arrived, Polly (a sprightly female aged about 60) was prudently kept in her cage. Jim—being tender-hearted as well as incredibly handsome— decided to let her out. This kindly action Polly has repaid by kissing Jim frequently, by taking a vast, if painful, liking to the family Alsatian, and by hoarding unto herself the bar-space between the far wall and the flap-hinge. Woe to the untaught customer who places his beer upon Polly's private deck. One malignant eye is bent upon this shocking liberty and the pirate tankard is smartly scuppered over the side. With a quick return to her usual unruffled composure Polly then paces her bridge, laughing like anything and mouthing suggestive, and highly unladylike, parrotries.

Bed and breakfast in this delightful pub is 25/-. And I have never tasted sandwiches more delicious than Jim's toasted chicken-and-mushroom with plenty of pepper at 2/6d.

The main hotel is the GRAND on the Esplanade (bed and breakfast from 45/-). Due to recent management—the female half of which was Nordic—the Danish invasions of Tynemouth, during which they destroyed the church of St Oswald built in A.D. 640 and generally tried to ruin the place, have been perpetuated in the Viking Restaurant (dinner by candlelight from 15/6d), and the Troll Bar. There are a considerable number of other magnificent bars, the most popular with the *cognoscenti* being the Buffet Bar. The Troll Bar, however, is a North of England manifestation well worth amazed inspection. It is what is known as a 'Moonlight Bar', a type much frequented by the teenager since it not only houses a juke-box but is also lit by a to me unbelievably ugly form of ultra-violet ray. This is said to cause nylon to become completely transparent and it certainly does something extremely odd to all white garments. The place appears to be peopled by a lot of ambulatory shirt-fronts and a collar and cuff or two, brightly picked out in pale mauve amid the encircling gloom.

An idea which might well recommend itself to London pubs, since it appears less old and curly and takes up less room than the permanent sandwich-counter lurking under fly-blown Perspex, is the trolleyful of fresh-cooked sausages, chicken legs, and huge seawater-plump mussels which is wheeled into the teenagers' bar at intervals.

Before we leave Tynemouth, special mention should be made of the TYNEMOUTH SAILING CLUB, not only because of the hardy determination of its members—both men and women—to launch themselves precariously on to the vasty deep in all weathers, summer and winter, but also because they are commendably patient with beginners—as long as the aforesaid beginners are of a type likely to enhance the cheerful atmosphere of the club-house. Or, at worst, not likely to ruin it.

Most members of the club work in Newcastle, which means they are able to put out to sea almost every evening at around 6.0 p.m. An idea which, to the Londoner blundering and tacking around in a restricted area of the Thames at Hampton on Sundays, seems almost like Neptune—to his delighted surprise—finding himself in Valhalla.

The road back to Newcastle from Tynemouth at night is breathtakingly beautiful. This particular road was my first introduction to the transformation from the ordinary, or even downright ugly, of nearly all North-Eastern coast roads after dark. Suddenly across the water the pipes, chimneys, cranes and boats loop themselves into a necklace of turquoise and gold lights against an ink-blue sky, shining comfortingly all along the edges of the rivers and the sea. An exact, if decidedly less expensive replica of, say, Cap Ferrat viewed at midnight from the heights above Monte Carlo.

46

North Shields

I don't even know what North Shields looks like by day. I only know that the view from the Fish Quay at night—of the lights of South Shields on the opposite bank reflected in the thickly lapping water—is the view I most long to see again.

North Shields appears not to have attached unto itself much history. Its name derives from the fishermen's huts, called 'shiels', which until comparatively recently were pretty well all the town consisted of.

It has its 'Wooden Dolly', a rather battered life-size model of a Cullercoats fishwife in full regalia. It also has a ghost.

The story goes that a house in North Shields was occupied many years ago by an old couple named Fafty who were very poor. One night their daughter brought to them a young sailor in search of lodgings who (rather foolishly as it turned out) displayed before them the gold and jewels he had collected on his travels. In the middle of the night these undisciplined old dears murdered the boy and hid his sea-chest. It wasn't until breakfast the next morning that they learned from their daughter that the sailor had been their long-lost son, Jim, who had run away to sea years beforehand and had now returned with the intention of lightening their old age and surprising them mightily. Without question he certainly managed the latter intention if not the penultimate one.

It is said that the spirit of Jim now haunts the area in the shape of a black Newfoundland dog. I must say that I find this a very daunting thought. There are so *many* large black dogs all over Northumberland, all followed by men going to the Local.

One can imagine a Northumbrian being filled with dismay at the sight of poor Jim unexpectedly resurrected in human form in the middle of tea, but the sight of any black Newfoundland dog would merely remind him of his Newcastle Brown Ale. Patting dogs which aren't there is apt to be faintly appalling— or so I am told by a cross-section of my more delirious acquaintances—but I have never noticed a Northumbrian actually *patting* a large black dog. They just follow them to the Local and then follow them home again. So almost any man around North Shields may have been following the unquiet spirit of an ill-starred sailor for weeks under the impression that this was merely man's best friend in quest of a ship's biscuit.

North Shields is almost a continuation of Tynemouth but it is completely different. For a start it contains the exotic, faintly notorious 'Jungle Club'. This is much frequented by the deep-sea fishermen who live in the area, earning up to £60 a week while at sea and then returning home to spend it before going to sea once more.

Before we go any further I must explain to the Londoner what I mean by deep-sea fishermen. While toying disgustedly with a morsel of bug-eyed cod, has it ever occurred to you by whose hand this by now suspiciously sauce-masked delicacy has reached you? Do you imagine your fisherman in the guise of a piscatorial old salt, brushing loose scales and dandruff alike from the inside of his hoary palm before lifting a pint of old-and-mild to a brine-flecked tooth?

It was Jean—the sweet and jolly barmaid from the upstairs bar of the Tyne-Tees pub, the 'Egypt Cottage' in City Road, Newcastle—who took me to 'The Jungle'. Having been fore-warned of its dangerously exciting reputation I looked around it with caution and misgiving.

"Dear God!" I exclaimed, "Who are those *gorgeous* beasts?" It was as if masculinity itself in all its pristine glory had decided to converge upon 'The Jungle' on that particular evening. Everywhere I looked some absolutely *fabulous* hunk of male was disporting himself with rippling muscles at the ready.

Jean looked surprised. "Fishermen," she said.

At risk of sending 32 whinnying biology teachers flat-chested down to North Shields for the duration of their summer holidays

Near-empty beaches at Warkworth

Bar in an old monastery, Blanchland

Walkers in the Northumberland National Park

Berwick-upon-Twee

I will here and now categorically state that until you've seen the fishermen of England you haven't lived.

Take Alan Kelly . . . John Mills personified in the days when I (and John Mills) was young.

Perhaps I ought to add that British fishermen like Alan Kelly will either like you or they won't. It takes them about ten seconds to make up their minds and, if they do like you, then they'll fight a mob on your behalf and, furthermore, they'll win. I have never been so anxiously watched over, so warmly entertained. But then . . . to Alan Kelly . . . I was just a strange old lady, dangerously playing with fire.

The boats they sail from North Shields are 'cobles' and Seine-boats. The former is pronounced 'cobbles' and the latter use 'Seine-nets' for white fish. Whinnying biology teachers should remember two things about deep-sea fishermen. It is considered bad luck to take a woman aboard and very bad luck indeed to be waved away from the quayside at the start of a long sea trip by any female person in whom you have the slightest romantic interest.

Bad luck having thus been avoided, an average of 15 men proceed to spend about three weeks around the coasts of Iceland or Greenland, working up to 24 hours a day once the fishing starts. They certainly earn their money. Deep-sea fishing is, they say, very boring. And these fishermen are not only sailors, able to do any Merchant Navy job; they also have to take on the chores a woman would do if it weren't bad luck to have them aboard. As Alan Kelly said, "We fetched in a million-and-a-half meals for Britain last time I was out. And I must have filleted a million of them."

Fishing now from North Shields is the *Stamilla*, a Polish vessel which arrived seeking political asylum. The Northumbrians watched from the quayside the evening she arrived. "They were making a great whambly mess of tying up," they recollect. "So we said, 'Come on you b . . . . .s. Better let *us* do it.'"

And do it they did.

Down The Mine

In keeping with my own tenet that everybody should go down a mine to see for themselves what it's like, I drove on a beautifully sunny morning to ASHINGTON; which as every World Cup football fan knows was the birthplace of Bobby and Jackie Charlton. It was bound to be a beautiful sunny morning. I was spending the day underground. Just as it is bound to be a day of severe sub-tropical storms and bottomless airpockets any time I am persuaded against my will that it would be more comfortable for me to fly anywhere.

On the way to Ashington I stopped in the little mining town of BEDLINGTON, where those rather bald terriers come from. Once the somewhat far-flung property of the Bishops of Durham, Bedlington is pretty, with wide grass-bordered streets. Its church, St Cuthbert's, is one of the many in which rested the bones of the saint on their journey from Lindisfarne.

On a rebuilt portion of this church is inscribed 'Watson's Wake 1669' in memory of Cuthbert Watson, a noted somnambulist. Waking one cold February night at the sound of a yell of warning Cuthbert was horrified to find himself halfway up one of the church buttresses wearing nothing more pious than a nightshirt. At which he let go of the church buttress, pitched to the ground, and died immediately.

In the churchyard too is a terse little tombstone which states:

"Poems and epitaphs are but stuff;
Here lies Robert Barras, that's enough!"

Succinct, certainly.

Bedlington is associated in many people's minds with the Miner's Picnic held in June. Everybody dresses up in his best, colliery bands play, flags are waved, and speeches are made. And a gigantic amount of beer is consumed.

In Ashington, the little red back-to-back houses are set in straight rows from First Street to Eleventh Street, each house facing its coal-bunker and one-time outdoor earth closet on the other side of the road. A single-track rail once ran down the middle for the small horse-drawn truck which delivered free coal in the morning and came back to empty the closets on the night-shift. Each house has its double door, somewhat like a stable door, for opening the top half and gossiping over—and also its well-hollowed sandstone sill for sharpening the carving knife. Everything is spotlessly clean and brightly painted—particularly the 'Back Ends', little built-on extensions which are the private property of the rent-free tenant. Outgoing tenants bargain fiercely with incoming tenants for the 'Back End' and if the price required is not met, then down goes the 'Back End' and that's the end of it.

But things, they say, aren't what they were. There is still no class-consciousness, everybody knows everybody else, they go to the same schools, still order their milk by a system of crosses on the wall. Now, however, modern flats are being built, robbed of the gossipy half-doors, and the younger generation own cars and live outside the town. Ashington is only three miles from completely unspoilt sea-coast and not far from the beautiful countryside around Morpeth. And so this one-time closed community breaks up a little more year by year.

The colliery is also only 5 minutes from one of the most enchanting little villages in Northumberland. BOTHAL, on the edge of the Wansbeck, is difficult to find unless you know it's there, down a steep hill lost amid trees and thick hedges. Its name derives from the Saxon 'bottell', an abode, and I personally can think of no more contented a place in which to abide, curling as it does peacefully around its 13th-century church and impressive small castle, built 600 years ago. The Barony of Bothal was in the hands of the Bertram family prior to 1166, and in 1343 Robert de Bertram obtained permission from Edward III to 'kernellate his manse' there and to build the castle. Thereafter the property passed, at the disposal of heiresses various, through the hands of Cavendishes, Hollises (Dukes of Newcastle), and Earls of Oxford and Mortimer to the Dukes of Portland, who still own it but have let it off to local industry for the entertainment of visitors from abroad. I must say that I am enthusiastically in favour of this. How educational for Europeans—still too often so very sniffy about England—to spend a weekend in such lovely surroundings. The Wansbeck ripples over stepping-stones at the foot of the castle and is spanned by a delicate old swingbridge. The banks are clustered with laburnum; and deer and badger are frequently seen to be less startled in these parts than are the visitors from abroad.

The miner is completely different from the fisherman or the countryman. He is very large, extremely tough, somewhat shambling. He enjoys football, quoits, marbles and racing pigeons and he uses the French 'r'-sound, well rolled into his throat. On the other hand when he's going home he will say "gang yem" which is more likely to have come from his Scandinavian ancestors.

So it might quite easily be very difficult to understand what he says. All he said to me, however, was "Hello Hen!" followed by "Hi Joe!" or "'Lo Jim!" depending upon who was accompanying me at the time. Not—mind you—just the once. No. Round every coal-face, in and out of the enormous machine shops containing one corner for four railway locomotives, up and down in the cage to the workings, and in the canteen at lunchtime, exactly the same man would repeat "Hi Joe!", "'Lo Jim!", "Well Skipper?", or "Ta ta Hen if'n I doan see you!"

Northumberland is probably the most famous coal-producing area in the world and 89 million tons have been mined at Ashington since the first shaft was sunk in 1867. Mining apprentices nowadays go through an intensive 3½-year training including courses at special centres for at least 10 weeks, learning safe methods of working and travelling below ground before being allowed down the mine.

I can't tell you exactly what conditions are like below ground because I was only taken 528 feet down a Training Mine. And I can't tell you what it feels like to be the Queen, or Princess Margaret and the Earl of Snowdon all decked in white, because all the gear I got was a beige overall. I did however get the proper headwear, and after bashing my skull extremely heavily three or four times before even going down in the cage I was pretty grateful for that. At the end of my inspection I was allowed to meet the fat, frisky pit ponies trotting all by themselves back to their stalls (and the only pathetic thing about a pit pony is his mane and tail cropped to undignified shortness for safety's sake) then suddenly I was rushed anxiously back through the workings to reach the cage before the men came off shift. It was only at that point I learned that it was not because of possible danger that I had not been allowed down a proper working mine. It was because the Northumbrian doesn't swear in front of women and somebody might have slipped up in the dark. Which was rather sweet of them, I thought.

In any case the trip was fascinating and not very frightening so long as one didn't remember all that heavy thickness of rock just above one's suddenly rather fragile pit-helmet. One certainly learned what is meant by a pit-prop. Pit-props were, for that particular $2\frac{1}{2}$ hours, the most important and interesting objects I'd ever seen in my life.

I had a chat with *one* miner though. It was a very pithy dissertation on the subject of death. "If ye're ganna gaen ye're ganna gaen," he opined. And went cheerfully into the modern 2-storey bath-house for a shower.

Not so long ago any miner on the early morning shift would turn back if he met a woman on his way to work. Like the fisherman, the miner thinks (possibly only too plausibly) that women are bad luck. Now however—though he may still think women are bad luck—he isn't so likely to be superstitious as well. Mining these days is being done more and more by remote control and electronics. Roof supports which once had to be moved by a man lying dangerously flat on his stomach, are self-advancing. Absolutely colossal machines called Continuous Miners also advance, like horrible, twisting, tortured, soulless monsters with vast jaws cutting and tearing their way through 20 feet of coal-seam a minute. These metal *tyrranosauri* are worked by one man and leave in their wake, thrown contemptuously down behind them, the coal ready to be carted away. The apprentice has to learn to control and understand these modern machines. Unless you're a trained mechanic there isn't much you can do about a Continuous Miner if he suddenly decides to go broody in a 9 feet by 6 feet space underground.

I wonder if the tedious London City worker realises that when he emerges from *his* Underground he spends the rest of the day amid a miasma of lung-corroding fumes whereas when the so-pitied miner emerges from underground (frequently at around lunchtime, depending upon his shift) he walks out into the purest fresh air? But there is just one thing about miners which would surely put the London City worker off trying mining. When the miner gets home at the end of the week he hands over his pay-packet to his wife. Unopened.

One of the most enjoyable evenings I spent in Northumberland was put on specially for me by the miners from the BACKWORTH Working Men's Club—a palatial edifice in the middle of what is termed 'the coalfields' near SEATON SLUICE.

It was arranged by Joe Bennett, wizard accordionist and dedicated upholder of fast-disappearing Northumbrian folklore and tradition. Firstly I was introduced to the Northumbrian Small Pipes by Colin Caisley who played for me the 'Border Fray' and the 'Keel Row'. In the Middle Ages, Small Pipes were used on both sides of the Border and the Scottish Bagpipes were later developed from these. But the Northumbrian sticks to his harmoniously richer, infinitely more melodious instrument which is worked not by blowing a terrible muzzein wail into a hapless tartan bladder but by working with the elbow a small pair of bellows attached to the waist by a leather belt. The Small Pipes bag is always of black and white Houndstooth check woven at Otterburn Mills. It is a further tradition that the miner's son accompanies him on the fiddle, so Colin's son, Nichol, then joined him in a lively 'Lamshaw's Fancy' before Jim Bryan played (with a virtuosity truly heart-catching) Schiller's 'Hymn To Joy' just to prove that what you cannot possibly do on the Scottish Bagpipes Jim actually *can* do on the Northumbrian Small Pipes.

But the highlight of the evening was a Northumbrian Sword Dance—not executed by a posse of dainty-toed caber-tossers delicately picking their way around crossed blades. These 'swords' were double-handled 'rappers' held aloft by five young miners executing figures just as complicated but much more virile. The step is the 'Rant', a sort of hob-nailed tap-dance which takes two years to perfect and seven minutes to execute. Nobody ever lets go of his end of the 'rapper' (not unless he can afford pints all round) excepting at a given moment when the 'Fixie' in the middle gets left with the lot miraculously arranged in wheel formation.

Norman Nesbitt, Joe Oxley, David Pearson, Colin Blewitt, Jack Kirtley—not one likely lad let go of his end of the 'rapper' at the wrong moment, not even as each one flung himself into a perfect backward somersault over the blades.

This, The Royal Earsdon Sword Dancers, is the only miners' team still extant keeping up the traditional form of Northumbrian dance, which dates from the religious celebrations of the Winter Solstice and is attended by a 'Tommy' and a 'Betty' to ward off evil spirits. Mr Guthrie Gibson was being a fairly decorous 'Betty' but the 'Tommy' was my friend 'Nibs', a miner of the old school who not only called the steps but was also finally quite unable to resist jumping up and down, doing his own perfectly-executed 'Rant' off-stage.

Oh golly! Nobody who knows me well ever takes me to the Changing of the Guard without also taking a large supply of highly absorbant tissues, 'Land of Hope and Glory' reduces me to hopeless sogginess any time I hear it; I didn't dare face anybody for a full week after the Trooping of the Colour, and I cry simply buckets at Lords even although I absolutely loathe cricket. What was I to do now? These boys were so *good*, so well trained, so entirely *unsung*. You *can*not just simply burst into floods of tears right in the middle of a Working Men's Club. So I took a large swig of my Newcastle Brown Ale and pretended to choke to death instead.

The evening ended with Eileen Brennan singing 'Blow the Wind Southerly' without benefit of microphone and so beautifully that she jolly nearly set me off again. Luckily, however, she followed this with 'Pretty Polly Perkins' which my friend Nibs assures me is a traditional Northumbrian song pinched by the colliers plying the canals to take coal to Paddington Green.

Well that's what my friend Nibs told me anyway. And if you knew Nibs like I know Nibs you would, like me, unquestioningly believe whatever Nibs said.

Touring Northumberland

By car, coach, or on foot, whichever way you travel and whichever road you choose to take, the coast and countryside of Northumberland are a constant surprise and delight. Bleak heather moor, warm sunny village, high crag, soft hillside, pine forest, small harbour, market town—all appear unexpectedly. The following chapters describe three car trips which I personally much enjoyed and of which, as we go, I shall be giving a little historical background and some possibly useful local information.

But Northumberland has a distinct tendency to tempt one from the way one meant to go, just a little way up this small track, just a minute or so up that attractive-looking hill to see what's on the other side. So that—in fact—you and I may not be together long.

In any case, if you have the time, it would be a pity to rush these beautiful drives through in one rubbernecking day. You will need to know where to stay if we should lose each other early on and you will also want a historical background to the places you may find yourself in after ignoring my instructions.

Absolutely essential is the Northumberland County Council Handbook and Register of Accommodation, price 2/6 (postage 4d) from Harold Hill & Son Ltd, Killingworth Place, Gallowgate, Newcastle upon Tyne. Without this booklet one is not only likely to miss half a dozen historical sites at times when they may be visited. One is also unlikely to be aware that fascinating annual local events such as the Warenford Sheep Dog Trials or the Alwinton Agricultural Show are going on practically right under the bonnet of the car.

Write also to Vaux Breweries, Sunderland, for their 'Hotels Which Bear the Sign of the Swallow', which gives names, addresses, telephone numbers, tariffs, photographs, and short descriptions of all their hotels in the North-East. I have naturally not visited them all but the ones I did visit were outstanding.

In addition it would be well to take with you Arthur Mee's 'Northumberland' in The King's England series. This gives a concise history in alphabetical order of every town and village of the slightest interest, covering the whole area. It costs 25/-.

Each of the following drives starts from and returns to Newcastle. And I hope that, as you go, you will find it possible to discover the subtle colours incorporated in what is popularly imagined to be the 'grey' stone in which most of the houses and cottages are built. After a while spent in Northumberland, and County Durham too, red brick seems terribly vulgar and unimaginative and red roofs are only attractive if they happen to be the pantiles of Berwick-on-Tweed.

I hope too that you will come to appreciate the bright green of the tree-bark, the peat-brown of the rivers and streams, and the trusting manner in which the villagers plant spring and summer flowers outside their cottage walls and all over their village greens for the delectation of the passer-by as well as of themselves.

You will travel for miles and be much more likely to see an astonished pheasant across your path than another car. You will never see a rude hoarding advising you either to stuff a reluctant wild animal into your petrol-tank or to subsist on a windy diet of milk, eggs, beans, and gravy-browning. If you lose your way nobody will assure you that you "can't miss it"—they'll be terribly anxious on discovering you already have. And if you break down somebody is bound to come along eventually, commiserate deeply, and take you either to the nearest garage or home to meet the rest of the family.

Northumberland National Park Drive

"What," I have asked of the Londoner, "is a National Park?"

"It is," he has replied, "a large area in South Africa reserved for the protection of Game Wardens."

"Or," he has added, "something."

In fact we have ten National Parks, covering over 5,200 square miles—or 9 per cent—of England and Wales. Two-and-a-bit of these National Parks are in the North-East. General information about them may be obtained from the National Parks Commission, 1, Cambridge Gate, Regent's Park, London N.W.1. Town dwellers aiming to be popular in National Parks should also ask for a copy of the Country Code.

To get to the Northumberland National Park take the road to Edinburgh which goes over Carter Bar to Jedburgh, and which is prettier than the A.1. This takes you to Belsay with its charming row of arcaded shops and a castle built from the stone quarried out of the old workings behind it. The Hall is still the seat of one of the few pre-Conquest families left in Britain—the Middletons. On Belsay Craig, to the south of the Hall, is a tree known as 'Silky's Seat' where a witch is wont to crouch, rocking in the winds and listening to the storms and the sound of the waterfall running into the lake.

Digress a bit from here, because nobody should miss CAMBO—the home of the Trevelyans (who it is said still dress for dinner every evening), whose estate, Wallington Hall, is now the largest National Trust acquisition in England, covering 20 square miles. The grounds were laid out by Capability Brown, who went to school in Cambo, and the gargoyles on the tiny estate bridge are from the old gates of the City of London, brought here in

58

Trevelyan ships. About a mile away is one of the most beautiful examples of estate villages in Britain, wonderfully neat and tucked away amid flowers and trees. In the bus shelter on the main road you may see a fleet of unattended bicycles attesting to the honesty of the local inhabitants. People from Cambo cycle to the bus-stop and then go to work, leaving their own machines in the shelter to be picked up again in the evening.

Now take the straight road to SCOTS GAP for about 5 miles through afforestation to your right and the Wallington Estates to your left. Watch for curlews along here and also for your first sight of grim WINTER'S GIBBET, which looks at its most dramatic standing starkly on the skyline as you approach the National Park boundary. Here, suspended in chains, swung the body of William Winter, who in 1791 with the help of two gipsy women murdered an old lady and removed her possessions on the back of a donkey he had calmly brought for the purpose. Nowadays it is said that chips from the gibbet are very good for toothache and I can only imagine that whoever made *that* particular odd discovery must have had pretty bad toothache. He had obviously walked all the way across intending to hang himself if it didn't work.

The road now runs across the moors with the SIMONSIDE hills to your right and a view straight ahead to the CHEVIOTS, dropping down into the valley of the REDE, where lies the village of ELSDON. It is said that the name derives from a Danish giant called Ella who had his stronghold on the Mote Hills, two man-made mounds on the east side of the Burn. The old pound for stray cattle may still be seen on the village green and the church is worth a visit. The Battle of Otterburn took place around here and in the 19th century over 100 skeletons were found packed closely into a mass grave, obviously victims of the battle. There is also an old Roman tombstone, found in 1809, with an inscription upon it which states "Julia Lucilla had this stone erected to her very meritorious husband, an inspector under the surveyor of the Flaminian Way, and a pensioner under the surveyor of the public works. He lived 47 years, 6 months, 25 days."

In Elsdon you will see your first pele-tower. Northumberland is famous for these small village fortifications now mostly converted into delightful private houses. The vault in this one

59

forms a drawing-room with walls 9 feet thick made of two 'skins' of stone filled with rubble. Once, at the first sign of trouble from marauders, the entire village was packed into these tiny little fortresses, with the cattle downstairs, the women and children on the first floor, and the men on the castellated roof defending the village.

On the other side of Elsdon is OTTERBURN but, before visiting the famous mills so attractive to American visitors in search of British tweeds, it might be well to stop at the Percy Arms Hotel for coffee, lunch, tea, dinner, or bed and breakfast, depending upon how long it took you to get here.

The mill is tiny and right out in the middle of the moor. Visitors are welcome from 9 a.m. until 5 p.m. daily (closed 12.30 to 1.30) and from 9 a.m. to 1 p.m. on Saturdays, from Easter to the New Year. The first record of a mill at Otterburn is in 1245, and in 1552 it was mentioned as being guarded nightly against the Scots. The sheds are filled with banks of foamy pastel wools hanging like cobwebs even from the ceiling. The most fascinating part of the process is the weaving; in a hut full of millions of bobbins where pretty young girls appear to be playing a medieval game of tennis, knocking the bobbins about on the looms to the tune of 'Poom-KA-Poom' and using what appears to be the only modern device on the premises—cheap little knitting counters to check their lines of colour. Heath-Robinson-type machinery rolls on thin rubber bands, wooden wheelbarrows trundle around, washing, pre-shrinking and spin-drying is done in an old shed with uneven and broken tiles on the floors, teazeling is accomplished with natural teazels planted like wheat-ears in large rollers. The result of all this is piled in bales of bright colour in a showroom the manager of which knows exactly how many dollars, schillings, pesetas or whatever to the pound and never makes a mistake. Everybody understands the snob-value of a genuine Otterburn Tweed and so do the mills. With the purchase of even just a skirt-length remnant you are also given an Otterburn Mill label to attach to the finished garment.

From here cross the GRASSLEES VALLEY, the greenest in the country, where at dawn and dusk you can see roe deer—cream and bronze, the size of a large dog—coming down to the Grasslees Burn to drink; and make for the banks of the RIVER COQUET, surely the most appropriate name for a merry, bubbling little riverlet. You will pass Dues Hill Grange where among the trees is a bastle-house, somewhat like a pele-tower but for members of the immediate family only. The woods around here are full of greeny-purple crested peewits and it's lucky I was with a couple of North Countrymen or I wouldn't have known what they were either.

The Coquet valley is particularly glorious in the autumn. Take the road to HOLYSTONE, stop at the Salmon Inn and walk up the footpath to the LADY'S WELL where once St Paulinus, whose statue stands in the middle of the well, is said to have baptised 3,000 people in one day. (A manifestation which must very much have resembled Oxford Circus underground station at 5.35 p.m. from Monday to Friday.) The pool is fed by a spring with crystal-clear water and the bottom is lined with quartz. It is surrounded by tall beech-trees and is now owned by the National Trust.

From here to HARBOTTLE, with the forbidding Harbottle Crags and a ruined castle behind it—and good bread-and-cheese and beer in the local pub. The roads turn pink around these parts, reminding the Londoner of The Mall. The reason the roads here remind the Londoner of The Mall is because the stone for The Mall came from Biddlestone Quarry just near ALWINTON.

Alwinton is 8 or 9 miles from CHEW GREEN, where a Roman camp remains, and was once the rallying point for sheep about to be driven over the Cheviots and into Scotland for sale. Clennel Street leading out of the town was a drove road but originated as a salt smugglers' track when salt was taxed in Scotland.

You are now in typical Cheviot country. Little copses of Scotch pines line the hillsides and the drystone walls are locked together without benefit of cement. Take the road to NETHERTON and ALNHAM, the source of the river Aln, where there is another pele-tower converted into a home. By now you will be driving along cart-tracks, through farm after farm, and it would be well to stop at one of them and ask your way to HEDGELEY GARAGE CAFÉ where the manager, Mr Norman Pringle, makes the best chips in Britain. "It's in the way you treat the oil. Keep it clean," he told me. If it's lunchtime, the café is a good place in which to have a good fresh pie or some bacon-and-eggs. If it's not any particular mealtime, at least take away some chips. They're *fabulous*. They'll also put you on your way down the

BREAMISH Valley to the hamlet of INGRAM where stands the National Park Information Centre. This houses live exhibits of bank voles, lizards, slow-worms, and a cross-section of river life in a large tank. Examples of otter, badger, and hedgehog spoors are provided for those who don't know what a greeny-purple crested peewit looks like either and there are also maps, charts, and photographs.

Drive up the road to the point where it ends and go on foot down a well-marked path from HARTSIDE to LINHOPE SPOUT, about 1½ miles of absolute silence except for the singing of the birds in the sunshine, the occasional hoarse skreek of a carrion crow (called locally a 'corbie') from his one large nest alone in a treetop, and the rippling of the cool shallow river over the stones. Many of the hills are crowned with Iron Age sites but personally I'd rather stay down here, lying in the grass, admiring the thick yellow, red-spotted monkey-musk, and thinking about how at this very moment 2,000 London buses are revving up and 800 road-drills are breaking down.

Take now the road back to POWBURN and drive down to ROTHBURY, a typical Border town and sheep-farming centre. Along the middle of the street is a narrow green, planted with chestnuts and elms. Point-to-points and steeplechasing take place on the racecourse which lies deep in the valley below the town.

But I do hope you go to Rothbury in the month of June, because it is then that CRAGSIDE, the home of Lord Armstrong, becomes the greatest attraction almost in the whole of Northumberland. I went there with my friend, Joe Gibson, and we drove through the Dunkirk Lodge Gate literally head-on into massed banks of rhododendrons of every colour you can possibly imagine and a great many you can't. They loomed above us and lay below us and curled around us as we drove for miles, and miles . . . and miles along a one-way track. It was the house Joe had wanted to show me, built in 1863, the first domestic building in the world to have electricity laid on by Swan, from Sunderland and a friend of the first Lord Armstrong. "We shall soon see the house," said Joe as we looped around another corner to see only more great deeps, and hills, and troughs, and crags covered in colour almost indigestible in its glory. We passed lakes and copses and pine trees . . . and rhododendrons. There were no other cars in sight, nobody, just Joe and me and the rhododendrons. Half an hour passed and then we saw a sign saying 'Short Cut To Way Out'. By this time I was beginning to feel that I'd seen my all-time rhododendron. I wasn't even sure any more that I *liked* rhododendrons. Joe wasn't sure either. We were glad we had taken the 'Short Cut'. Ten minutes later we decided to change the subject. Joe produced an aural thesis on the merits of Booth's 'High & Dry' Gin and I responded with an enthusiastic description of a trip I once took to Lithuania. We snaked round and round, on and on, knowing by now that it would never end and both privately wondering what we were going to tell our parents.

We plunged into forests of firs from which we got views of artificial 'top-lakes', and the roofs of old houses with slats like wafer-biscuits. We passed little bridges, forget-me-nots, rock outcroppings, baby-green beech-trees. We rushed blindly back into banks, dips, dells, and dingles full of those rhododendrons, thick enough to walk on. We saw last year's bracken, this year's bracken, and next year's bracken. And we never once retraced our drive.

Suddenly, without the slightest warning, it was all over. There was the house, a huge edifice standing as if carved out of the rock around it, pregnant with gables, turrets, oak beams, flying buttresses, gargoyles, pantiles, wooden nails, and timbers; a mixture of periods, styles and architectural eccentricities reminding me somewhat of the 'Ivory Castle' advertisements put out in my youth by Gibbs' Dentifrice. It looked enormously rich, with huge chandeliers just visible through curtains lined and double-lined. The morning view over lake, pines, and—(Booth's 'High & Dry' and Lithuania now suddenly forgotten)—rhododendrons, seemed almost gloriously unfair.

And, at the kitchen door, was a little slate. '2 pints please' was all that was required the day Joe and I were there. Which, after *all* those rhododendrons, did seem such an anti-climax, even just for breakfast.

After this bemusing, if not-to-be-missed, experience it is well to call at the Angler's Arms at WELDON BRIDGE before going back to Newcastle. This is a very attractive hotel, well known for good food, and so long as you refrain from saying 'rhododendrons' to them and remember to call it 'Booffs' in proper Northumbrian fashion, they'll serve you a 'High & Dry' as an aperitif.

Roman Wall and
South Northumberland Drive

For this drive take with you the Northumberland County Council leaflet 'The Roman Wall' which you can obtain free from the Central Library (see page 27), since it includes an easily-understood chart of the route. It would really also be a good idea to take J. Collingwood Bruce's 'Handbook to the Roman Wall' (price 15/-) because, even if you didn't have time to study it before leaving, it contains an excellent index.

For those who have had no time to read Collingwood Bruce, a short description of the Roman Wall as it once was will at least help them to understand what they're looking at.

The Roman Emperor Hadrian designed this bastion (in the words of Professor Sir Ian Richmond) 'to abolish vagueness, forswear expansion, and consolidate the Empire behind firmly fixed frontiers.'

The Wall was 80 Roman miles long, stretching from Wallsend to Bowness on the Solway. At every mile (1,620 yards) stood a milecastle, and two watchtowers were built between one mile-castle and the next. Each milecastle was about 60 feet × 75 feet in area with doors on both North and South walls. They accommodated about 50 men in small central barracks and these men patrolled the walls and watchtowers. The watchtowers were about 14 feet square inside and were used for purposes of defence and for sending messages along the length of the entire fortifications.

On the North side of the Wall was a ditch about 27 feet wide and 9 feet deep, and on the South was an earthwork called the Vallum set about 80 yards from the Wall. The Vallum consisted of a ditch 20 feet wide and 10 feet deep with 20 feet-high mounds of earth on each side, the whole measuring about 120 feet across.

If possible, it is a good idea to make two visits to the MUSEUM OF ANTIQUITIES in the quadrangle of the University of Newcastle, by the Haymarket, in connection with the Roman Wall. Before going on this particular drive, visitors should see the model of the wall on the first floor of the museum. But it is more satisfactory to have seen the Wall itself before inspecting the Roman antiquities and the full-scale reconstruction of the Mithraeum, which are on the ground floor.

Your first sight of the Roman Wall is as you leave Newcastle via HEDDON-ON-THE-WALL along the Military Road. This was built and opened in 1751, after General Wade set out from Newcastle in 1745 to intercept Bonnie Prince Charlie at Carlisle. He failed to get there due to inability to get his artillery over the bad roads, though the arrowlike quality of the present design stems from the original Roman idea of defence through speed of movement.

As you drive along through valley farmland, looking at the Wall striding along over the hills to your right, your main feeling should be of humble amazement at this fantastic feat of engineering. There is an awareness of mysterious forces, only just intangible; of something still going on which is only just out of sight. The whole effect has been so carefully preserved, so completely unspoiled. I was suddenly reminded of revisiting Polperro in Cornwall, still expecting to find the dear little fishing village tucked away amid the rocks I knew so well before the war. But this was 1963, and to my utter revulsion I was greeted at the harbour-entrance by a tall, thin, very sad man dressed as an etiolated piskie—bells and all—bearing in one hand a wooden placard inscribed 'Welcome to Polperro'. I left precipitately and never went back. I am happy to say that the wise Northumbrians have stoutly resisted any temptation to patrol the wall with splay-footed pseudo-Centurions hawking ice-cream, plaster Hadrians, mock Roman coins, and/or hot dogs.

On your way to CHOLLERFORD you will cross DERE STREET at STAGSHAW CROSSROADS. Dere Street ran through the Wall to the North, proving that although the Wall was built to keep out the barbarians, commerce was still carried on with some of them. This is where you should start noticing the ditch and where you also get a wonderful 30-mile view of the Cheviots. Shortly after this the outlines of the Vallum are also plainly visible.

At CHOLLERFORD BRIDGE, stop for coffee at the George. If, on the other hand, you should stay here the night you can fish for trout for your breakfast from the SIMONBURN which runs at the edge of the garden. This is a particularly entrancing little spot, with its tracery of delicate leaves forming a halo around the green bark and the mossy bridge.

Inside the hotel is a strangely-placed sash window over the lounge fireplace and opposite the entrance is a house most skilfully constructed from a disused railway station.

From here you must visit CHESTERS Roman Fort and the Museum, noting on your way there the lovely Vanbrugh-style Riding School built to Norman Shaw's design.

Chesters—or CILURNUM—was a large fortress capable of housing a 500-strong cavalry regiment. It was built in the 2nd century and is actually on the Wall. The outlines of barracks, defences, stables, Headquarters, the house and baths of the Commandant, and the regimental bath-house are still visible.

From here drive into the Northumberland National Park and stop at LIMEHOUSE BANK for a view of the entire North Tyne valley and the coastal plain.

A little further on there is a lay-by to the right behind which is a pile of boulders with which the Romans had obviously intended to form part of the ditch. They then, for some reason, abandoned the project. This is where you get a first true impression of the whole countryside, full of treasures left thrillingly unguarded for anybody to discover. These particular boulders show quite clearly the wedge-marks made for the purpose of splitting the stones into flat casings.

Not far away, and to the left of the road at CARRAWBURGH is the sign for BROCOLITIA where a short walk up the springy turf will take you to the MITHRAEUM—in my opinion the most exciting and fascinating find of all. This 3rd-century temple stands beyond the South-West corner of the fort. Of the three fine examples of Roman altar-stones there, the most marvellous is the Mithraic statue, built with a little shelf at the back for a lamp placed to shine through the small holes carefully carved around the head. This is the Mithraeum which is reconstructed in the Museum of Antiquities in Newcastle, in a small theatre off the main room. A taped 8-minute running commentary is given there, and this is much easier to understand after seeing the original.

Drive on to HOUSESTEADS and walk up by a field path from the road to the large fort of BORCOVICIUM capable once of housing 1,000 infantry. This fort was also inserted in the Wall itself. The systems for underfloor heating and drainage can easily be seen. There are also outlines of gateways, Headquarters, granaries and turrets. Under the stones here were discovered skeletons of people who must have died in peculiar circumstances since the Romans always buried their dead outside the populated areas. This section of the fort is thus gruesomely now designated 'The Murder House'.

There is an Information Centre at ONCE BREWED. The pub up the road is called the TWICE BREWED INN. Nobody seems to know the significance of these intriguing names, which is a pity because one feels certain it would be fascinating. Just past here and to your right you can walk to the top of the gentle slopes and see the reason why the Wall is built where it is. If you stand on the Wall at STEEL RIGG and look westwards towards WINSHIELDS you will get a good view of the sheer and terrifying drop on the other side. This view, apart from trees which have grown, is virtually the view the Romans saw, and you are now standing on the last outpost of the old Roman Empire, just like any other visitor from Singapore, Little Elk, or Vladivostock, and very few indeed from London as well.

Hadrian's Wall makes a bleak photograph and all too often the justly proud Northumbrian uses it to advertise the attractions of his land. So the drive down through lush foliage to GREENHEAD village is a pleasant surprise. From here you can see Thirlwall Castle built in the 14th century with stones from the Wall, as were many buildings hereabouts before such vandalism was arrested. The name derives from the fact that when the Picts made a breach in the Wall here they were said to have 'thirled' it. Nowadays, miners breaking through from one working to another call it a 'thirling'.

Right on the Western edge of the county is the village of GILSLAND and the sausages and pickles served by Ted and Joyce

Mason with fresh bread and butter at the Station Hotel. There is a proper dining room with a proper menu but you can still have 'steak minute' with peas, mushrooms, and tomatoes at the bar for 6/6d or grilled trout for 4/6d.

You can stay here too, and be made very welcome with electric blankets to every bed and a whopping great breakfast all round. In addition there's Tadge, the Border Terrier, and 150 yards of Hadrian's Wall and a bit of milecastle in the back garden.

Ted Mason, the manager, left London 13 years ago. He likes it better in Gilsland. For one thing there's no pomposity at the Golf Club, new members are made welcome, and you're not likely to get blackballed for humping your clubs round in your wife's shopping trolley. Which is what actually happened to one of Ted's friends at a marginal golf club in a small suburb off the Great Metropolis.

While you're there ask to see the charming 'Extract from Directory of Cumberland and Westmorland 1829'.

Gilsland, it states, "has been the favourite and fashionable resort of the votaries of *Hygeia* for nearly a century. Here the valetudinarian seeks re-invigoration, and the pleasurist society and its concomitant gaieties . . . The hotels afford every requisite accommodation and amusement, at a moderate expense, the charges for board and lodging being 7/-, 4/6d, or 2/6d per day for each person in the three different *classes* of visitors, who all mix together two or three nights a week in the assembly rooms, where rank has no influence in the choice of partners for the social dance."

Rather saucy that. Particularly as one gathers from the rest of the description that a large section of the visitors employed the main portion of their time in Gilsland plunging heavily into chalybeate springs in an attempt to cure a 'diversity of diseases'. So, with scenes of licence to shame Petronius going on two or three times a week between the different classes, one never knew *what* one might pick up.

Near Gilsland is the 'Popping Stone' where Scott is said to have popped the question to his future wife, Charlotte Carpenter. who lived at Wardrew House and who, it might be well to add, he did *not* meet in the assembly rooms.

Return by way of HALTWHISTLE and up the STANEGATE ROAD, the building of which preceded the Wall by 100 years

68

and which now leads straight through the middle of a typical Northumbrian farm in the centre of which is CHESTERHOLME MILESTONE. At the top of this is VINDOLANDA, a 4th-century fort which was not part of Hadrian's Wall but part of Agricola's defences in A.D. 78. From here you can glean a good idea of how the Romans could watch the hordes approaching down the hills, wrapped in sheepskin and looking decidedly fierce. This fort was occupied from the early 1st century to the end of the Roman era in the 5th century and shows transition from a military fort to a farm for part-time Roman soldiers.

Return to the main road which drops down to HAYDON BRIDGE, in the churchyard of which there is the following epitaph: "Here lyeth the body of M. Simon, who died on the 18th March 1710, in the 49th year of his age. During the last four years of his life he was tapped four times for dropsy, and three times he had taken away from him about MCCC pints of water. He bore his disease with wonderful resolution, and in the intervals of the tappings pursued his business with cheerfulness, and never dreaded the operations. He was remarkable for his amiability. He was an affectionate husband, sincere friend, and good neighbour . . ." The poor fellow certainly shipped an awful lot of water after he reached the age of 45.

This road takes you into HEXHAM, peaceful centre of the surrounding prosperous farmland. The Priory Church is one of the most splendid in England, built on land given in 674 by Queen Ethelreda to her favourite, Wilfrid. He built it with stones taken from Hadrian's Wall and dedicated it to St Andrew in memory of his visit to St Andrews on the Coelian Hill in Rome, where he went after studying under St Aidan at Lindisfarne.

All that is now left of this church is a fine Saxon crypt, the Saxon apse behind the choir, and St Wilfrid's Chair. The present church was rebuilt by the Augustinian Canons in the 12th century.

Hexham has had an unhappy history of bloodshed and battle but it is a quiet place now, and one to stay a while in and inspect with a good local history to hand. The narrow streets have delightful names such as Hencotes and Priestpopple, and there is a fabulous view over the Tyne valley from the top of the hill.

The colonnaded covered market—the largest in the North for

wool and cattle—is called (like so many in the North-East) the Shambles. Stay a day or so in Hexham if you have time. The small County Hotel in Priestpopple is extremely comfortable and is thickly populated with knowledgeable local farmers.

On the other hand, one of my favourite hotels in the district is in the tiny little rose-infested hamlet of BLANCHLAND not very far away. This is the luxurious and very interesting LORD CREWE ARMS, just over the small one-way bridge leading into this completely square village which was obviously built as one unit, since all the cottages blend perfectly with one another.

The Lord Crewe Arms is part of all that is now left of Blanchland Abbey and is built out of the kitchen and Prior's House. The bar is in the monastery crypt and the fireplace in the lounge with an escape hatch to the right of the chimney is the one mentioned in 'Devil Water' (see page 21). The bedrooms are perfectly lovely, with beamed ceilings and antique furniture, and there is part of the 14th-century Abbey glass in the Bamburgh Room windows.

This is Braes of Derwent Hunt country but don't try to join in if you normally only indulge yourself in mimsy old Shire stuff. These chaps are real pros and the country is extremely difficult. There is wonderful grouse-shooting over the moors if you are lucky enough to get invited, and if you aren't you can still gaze across the yellow gorse and purple heather from the window of your room. Or there's sailing and trout fishing on the Derwentwater reservoir and the river.

Gerry Coley, the manager, efficiently upholds the Vaux tradition, 'A meal at any time', and a single room is 35/- a day with continental breakfast 4/6d extra but no extras for early tea, morning paper, or bedroom heating. Weekly terms with full board are £23 and after a look at the brochure of which Gerry has a supply it seems almost churlish to stay less than a week. The booklet contains three walks around Blanchland, a history of the area, and of Hexham town and the Abbey, and a trip round Hadrian's Wall.

The return to Newcastle skims the edge of the glorious pine-shaded Derwent Reservoir—a bright blue lake, approximately three-quarters of a mile wide, set amid green fields with the purple and yellow moors in the background. If it's a fine day you'll be sorry if you came here without bringing a picnic.

Northumberland Coast Drive

You'll need a picnic for this one too—or at least you'll need a little frying pan and a 'Gaz' portable cooker. That's for when we get to CRASTER.

This is my favourite drive. Take the road from Newcastle to ALNWICK which announces its imminence from afar by means of the Percy Lion with flying tail atop its very tall column. The road into the town goes through the Hotspur Gate—indubitably the narrowest part of the A.1 between London and Edinburgh.

Don't rush through this lovely little town, the seat of the Percy family since Norman days. Alnwick Castle, the home of the Dukes of Northumberland, is open at certain times and well worth a visit, and you might even meet the Duke in Pink at the head of the Hunt. He's said to be a very nice man and he might even smile if you say "Good day!" He is much admired hereabouts.

If you'd rather have a drink try the pub locally known as the DIRTY BOTTLES because it has some dirty bottles in the window with a notice running thus: "These bottles have been here over 150 years. Whilst putting them here the man collapsed and died. It was said that if anyone tried to move them they would share the same fate. They have never been touched since." Shades of a lazy potman in all possibility but too late to risk disbelieving him now.

It was in Alnwick that I realised the exemplary care taken by all North-Easterners to serve good fresh food. The freshest possible bap-sandwiches were served to me there in a modest little place called even more modestly THE CORNER CAFÉ. The name alone is sufficient to conjure up in the Londoner's mind dirty cups of weak tea and flies in the ointment with which the stale buns are spread. As I asked for two more baps I praised their freshness and the surprised look on the manageress's face proved to me immediately that this little tearoom is only called 'The Corner Café because it's actually on the corner, not because they want to deter customers from entering it.

From here take the road which branches off to the left to CHILLINGHAM to see the fierce and famous herd of wild white cattle. As these are decidedly more dangerous than the sleepy, over-publicised Longleat lions it would be well to study page 22 of your Northumberland National Park Handbook (see page 58) before making the detour. Chillingham cattle are much bigger than domestic cattle, very fit, horribly agile, and apt to attack one if one should venture within their preserves without benefit of protection from the Keeper.

The origins of Chillingham Castle itself are somewhat vague. Part of it dates from the 14th century and Sir Jeffrey Wyntville, architect of Windsor Castle, apparently added to it in the 1820s. Honeyman describes the present building as a 'masterpiece of inconvenience'.

Under the balcony is preserved a 'Toad-stone' in which it is said a live toad was discovered enclosed in a small cavity when the castle was being built. Tomlinson, in his 'Comprehensive Guide to Northumberland', mentions that "In the Steward's Room close by there is a rude painting of the toad," upon which advice one's imagination is apt to shudder deliciously on the question of what the Steward saw.

The cattle are the only herd in the British Isles unfortified by domestic stock for over 600 years. When the wall was thrown round the park it encompassed them in their forest lair. They are ruled by a 'King' bull, and number only around 35 animals in all. In 1966 the 12-year-old 'King' bull died in a fight with an 8-year-old in which both had their necks broken. Thereafter a fierce battle for supremacy took place. The prize is an exclusive choice of cows since no male other than the 'King' is allowed near them for breeding purposes.

The 'King' only sires calves after the cows are two years old, and before the calf is born the cow leaves the herd and goes up into the hills. Ten days later the cow returns with her calf and the herd look it over. If it is found wanting in physique they push it away and she returns with it to the hills. She will bring it back 3 or 4 times at 14-day intervals but if it continues to be rejected she will eventually return alone, leaving her calf to die. Thus the stock is maintained, pathetic though the thought may be of the deserted and bewildered calf to us, the over-populated.

In Northumberland you can nearly always get a correct weather forecast, sometimes apparently entirely due to the particular stance of a bluebell. In Chillingham it will be bad weather if the herd are coming downhill away from the wind. How useful it would be if in London one could tell the prevailing winds by the peculiar behaviour of the number 11 bus. Whereas all one *can* tell in London is that the number 11 bus will invariably behave peculiarly, whatever the weather.

Return to the A.1 at BELFORD, where you will get your first view of HOLY ISLAND, 3½ miles long with the castle, village and priory all collected together at one end. Obviously you wish to drive on to the island but this isn't as easy as you might suppose. It is only safe to cross 3½ hours after one high tide and up to 2 hours before the next one. Dicing with these times not only threatens to wreck the car forever but also presupposes that one might have to spend 8 hours sitting in a little white box on top of a pole in the middle of the sea, while a handful of Holy Islanders, misanthropically muttering "Dom furriners!", make up their minds whether to come out and rescue one or not.

To find out about tides buy 'The Journal' which prints them every day. There is also a chart of tide tables at the entrance to the causeway.

To reach the island turn down by the Plough Hotel at BEAL and drive to the railway crossing on the edge of the sea.

Holy Islanders, so I was told, consider even the Northumbrian to be a 'dom furriner'. "You can't even go to the loo on the island without they know it," said a disgusted Novocastrian. Naturally therefore I was a little anxious as I drove along the excellent road which had suddenly appeared in perfect condition from under the sea. It wasn't that I wished particularly to go to the loo. It was that I hoped I *wouldn't* wish particularly to go to the loo. And everybody knows *that* feeling. I always get it when one of those newfangled jet-aircraft takes off with me inside it—due to the fact that I am unshakeably convinced

73

that if I tread upon the floor my foot will go through the bottom of the silver-paper holding it together.

I passed the SNOOK, a sort of pushed-together sand-dune upon which I am assured people not only actually live but also indulge in thriving salmon-fishery. Then I drove on to the island and had a look at the castle swooping and curling around on its rock as if actually a part of it. The original castle, built in 1550, was destroyed during the Jacobite Rebellion. In 1902 the ruins were bought by the owner of 'Country Life', quite obviously in a commendable effort to live *dans le vraie*, and restored for him by Sir Edward Lutyens.

After that I eyed the outside of the sheds in which now flourishes a recently-established mead industry. Liqueur and honey are also manufactured in this building but the whole idea seemed to me somewhat specious so I decided instead to go and look at the ruins of the priory of Lindisfarne, the cradle of Christianity in the North of England.

Here in A.D. 635 came St Aidan, a humble Celtic monk from Iona, at the invitation of King Oswald, to teach a new faith. From here he commenced the task of explaining understandable rudiments of Christianity to the Northumbrians. To the end of his life he remained completely uninfluenced by his friendship with kings, bishops and courtiers, and his history is worth more than cursory study. The ruins of the lovely priory are not, however, those of the church St Aidan built. He finally died at Bamburgh in 651, his head resting on the timbers of the one he erected there.

Here in 644 came St Cuthbert, most famous of all Northumbrian saints, and here he died in 687. It would be well to study Arthur Mee (see page 57) on the history of this priory, the splendid ruins of which are of the final rebuilding by the Benedictine monks of Durham in 1080.

The Lindisfarne Gospels, masterpieces of 7th-century art and craftsmanship, were illuminated by Eadfrith who became Bishop of Lindisfarne in 698. They were carried away with St Cuthbert's body in 875 when the Danes invaded, and fell into the sea, from which they were recovered at low tide. They are now on view under glass in the Manuscript Display Room of the British Museum and facsimiles are available for reading.

It was when I was walking away, just thinking, from the

priory that I came upon Walter McCulloch Hope. He asked me in for a cup of tea amid a pile of patchwork cushions of incredible imagination and virtuosity, in a little white pebble-dash cottage blessed with a view in contemplation of which no Londoner could fail to get homesick for the gasworks.

Walter is a native of Holy Island who worked on the railways in Newcastle. A pioneer of further education for adults he is an expert on the history of his own island. He it was who explained to me that the lovely name 'Lindisfarne' derived from Lindisfarne Dyke which in turn came from the Anglo-Saxon 'Lindisfarena Ealand' given to it by the Danes. He showed me fossilised vertebrae washed up on the beach and still supposed by many islanders to be 'Saint Cuthbert's Beads'. And he pointed proudly to the miles and miles of clean white sand upon which, on a particularly hot August Bank Holiday, "you might," he said, "find fully three families picnicking".

I eyed Walter—ruddy, black-haired, thick-sweatered, heavy-set, and corduroyed—as he started back to his gardening. He retired to Lindisfarne in December 1964. "How old are you now, Walter?" I asked.

"Over 70," he cautiously replied. And, defensively at my look of frank disbelief, "Well, it's very healthy here, you know. We had to shoot a man to start the cemetery."

"Whatever does the oldest inhabitant look like then?" I asked him.

"That's him there," said Walter pointing to an upright and sprightly figure turning into the square. I lumbered after the upright and sprightly figure. "I hear," I panted as I reached him, "that you're privileged to be the oldest inhabitant of Holy Island!"

A bright and highly offended eye was turned in my direction. "I *am* not!" emerged from a decidedly orotund larynx. "No! He deed laast week. Aam the *next* oldest!"

And off he strode on his several businesses.

As I passed Walter again he waved at me from out of the middle of his lupins and called: "Come back. Come back one day and stay overnight. We'll make a tour of the island!"

I will, Walter. Indeed I will. Who could resist such an un-wrung invitation from a native of a British island which 'doesn't like foreigners'?

And as I re-passed the Snook, now wrapped in unimaginable inky darkness, I suddenly remembered that I'd never once wanted to go to the loo after all.

From Holy Island make your way to BERWICK-ON-TWEED past HAGGERSTON CASTLE where the teenagers of the area come from miles around to dance in the ballrooms and drink coke in the dungeon bars. As you drive into the town you will probably notice that one of them has inserted (indelibly) 'pre-' in front of 'Historic Town of Berwick Upon Tweed' with which announcement the Council have decorated their boundary. But take no notice of that. Even the Council haven't.

As you drive into Berwick, England's most northerly town, you are firstly surprised at a sudden impact of red pantiles after the mimosa-and-mauve roofs sheltering most of Northumberland. Berwick is a walled town with its long military tradition now taken from it. The Vanbrugh barracks stand sadly devoid, by order of the government, of their colourful King's Own Scottish Borderers.

The *patois* is a little difficult to understand since it consists of part Northumbrian, part Scottish; indeed, Edinburgh is Berwick's centre of shopping and local commerce.

On the far side of the famous red sandstone bridge, built in the 17th century, is the firm of 'Cowe' established in 1801. This announces itself as the 'Home of the Original Berwick Cockles', delicious peppermint sweets, sold in a guarantee-wrapped tin, which were apparently great favourites with the late Princess Mary Adelaide of Teck. Even if you don't like peppermints as much as did Queen Mary's mother the shop is worth a visit if only because of its delightful lack of supermarketry. They retain their genuine old bentwood chairs still backed with blue enamel advertisements for 'NUBOLIC SOAP'—whatever *that* may have been in grandmother's day. The smell of the place suddenly brought to my mind my own grandmother's *femme de ménage* dumping her ample posterior on one such chair and requesting of the grocer such information as he felt inclined to divulge on whether or not he really considered he could pass off that lump of old candle-wax as fresh and genuine *Pont L'Eveque*?

Little old Berwick lanes lead into small courtyards and grassy squares littered with Elizabethan cannon. Street-names are honest and to the point. Foul Ford refers to a ford once used to cross the town sewer. Hide Hill, up behind the Town Hall, was once the market for the hides of the succulent 'Kylie Beef' still much in evidence in the Berwick butchers' shops.

Berwick sausages are the best in the world and may be bought in Hide Hill, the main street, or eaten cooked (if specially requested) in the turquoise-painted King's Arms to your right going uphill.

On the other hand if you want real thick *potage de la maison* as a first course, then try Sepp's Grill Bar.

The most fascinating thing to do in Berwick is to walk round the city walls on the beautifully-kept green lawns covering them. On the one side is a breathtaking view of the old town, on the other an equally breathtaking view of mile upon mile of sea coast. You will pass the perimeter of the Wool Market and a tanner's yard to reach the parish church, which is an odd shape, without tower or bells, because it was one of the only two churches to be built in Britain during Cromwell's Commonwealth. Curfew is still rung every evening at 8.0 from the Town Hall. The churchyard is, I think, particularly remarkable for the beauty of its old trees, thickly clustered, with barks green as the stem of a daffodil.

There is no sight in Northumberland more sad than that of the unfrocked pinky-grey barracks buildings seen from the town wall. So very quiet without the clashing colours of the uniforms, the sound of the pipes, staccato orders, and the spark of boot-nails. But as you reach the bright blue harbour and the docks, and the grass gives way to flagstones, you get your best view of Stephenson's Royal Border Bridge curving across the Tweed like a well-strung bow and you remember that you are only a visitor, primed merely to appreciate what still exists.

On your way to BUDLE BAY you are likely to see that Holy Island is by now right in the middle of the sea and cut off for the nonce from human contact. This may help you to understand why the Lindisfarnian is apt to fail occasionally to understand ·your complaints. This happens to *him* all the time.

When the tide is out, Budle Bay is full of wild swans, duck, pink-foot geese, and oyster-catchers.

The next village is the pride of Northumberland. BAMBURGH with its glorious castle appearing suddenly on the horizon; Lord

Armstrong's infinitely majestic stronghold, the place where the film of 'Becket' was made, and the hideaway to which it is said Lancelot carried Guinevere. This is 'King Ida's castle huge and square' which we used to recite from Scott's 'Marmion' when I was at school and which made just about as much sense to me at the time as having to intone 'Forgive us our trespassers' every morning at 9.0 when, insofar as I could recollect, we hadn't had a trespasser for months.

Bamburgh is the place from which Grace Darling, who was born there, rowed her coble to the rescue of the *Forfarshire* in 1838. In the churchyard is her impressive tomb and the Grace Darling Museum close by is a delightfully nostalgic welter of bonnets, a chair-cover knitted by her, and a letter from the proprietor of the Adelphi Theatre offering her £10 a week to appear on the London stage—an offer one presumes she smartly rejected.

The castle, pink in the sun on the edge of the blue-white beach, was built on the site of the one mentioned above and stands on the same seam of whinstone as does Hadrian's Wall. But the present Keep was only founded 500 years *after* Scott's 'huge and square' which partly accounts for my childish bafflement and also hauls poetic licence way beyond the realms of absurdity. Tomlinson's 'Comprehensive Guide to Northumberland' includes an excellently bloodthirsty history of the castle and a description of the fortunes of the present one, the building of which was in fact started by Henry I.

Another CASTLE, on the edge of the green, is a good spot for real boiled-beef-and-carrots and a pint of beer poured by Willy Graham. There are five letting rooms here as well; and you might also like to see Willy's 'patent no-fume ashtray' which appears to be achieved with a pint mug and an old domino.

SEAHOUSES just a bit down the coast is where I would like to spend a summer holiday—in the BAMBURGH CASTLE HOTEL right on the edge of the harbour. There are 20 rooms, and full board is only 16 guineas a week, which is why you have to hurry if you want to book one. Les Hunt, in partnership with Willy Graham of the Castle, is the director, manager, secretary, barman, and cellarman—though in the bar he has cheerful and pretty blonde Isabel to help him. This bar is an enormous room full to bursting with a wide smile from Les and with a view of

78

the blue blue sea, gaily coloured boats and nets, and Mr Crisp coming in for his 'nip' at 2.30 p.m.

Your pint is measured at the Bamburgh Castle Hotel by a 'beer meter'. "I've never seen a 'beer meter' in London," I said. "I've never seen *beer* in London," Les replied, pouring me another excellent measure. "People talk," he added, "of going up to London. What do they mean *up*? It's *down*."

With which perfectly true statement nobody can even begin to argue.

Regular trips are run from Seahouses to the bird sanctuaries on the FARNE ISLANDS, where it is extremely difficult to walk without treading on a guillemot, a puffin, a tern, or a baby seal.

Next comes BEADNELL, with a harbour actually facing West towards the Cheviots. This is a sailing centre, more sophisticated than the others, with weekend cottages along the seafront. The harbour is particularly colourful, with an old lime kiln on the edge surrounded by piles of lobster pots painted orange, emerald, and black. The cobles in the bay are turquoise and white, made fast to the bollards with orange ropes, and huge piles of crabs and lobsters are packed into boxes around you as you sit in this sun-trap thinking deliciously about nothing at all. Just outside the village is a blacksmith's forge. The smithy is a wrought-iron expert—each little leaf in his design grows straight off the stem and 'Boo' to him is a far politer insult than 'Weld'. On your way to EMBLETON you will also pass TUGHALL GRANGE, a perfect example of the Northumberland gracious country home where the Percy Hunt may meet for a stirrup cup while Jack the Shepherd blows his nail, doffs his cap, sings hey-nonny and generally feels a jolly sight better off than you do.

At Embleton I do hope it's teatime. Because at the DUNSTAN-BURGH CASTLE HOTEL tea consists of lettuce and cucumber sandwiches, scones and jam, and home made cakes for 3/6d. Opening time in the bar is cushioned with the usual upholstered elbow rest. Or you can stay overnight for 30/- and use the private beach hut next day.

From Embleton one may admire the gigantic ruin of DUNSTAN-BURGH CASTLE which was built by the Earl of Lancaster, son of Henry III. There are coloured quartz crystals to be picked up around here called 'Dunstanburgh Diamonds'. These are supposed to form part of an immense treasure some captive wench in a crystal tomb guarded by two skeletons will present to her deliverer. However it would perhaps be as well to warn the unwary that the last chap who tried this is immortalised in a poem by William Gill Thompson. Not only does one verse run somewhat dizzily thus:

> "And now they go both high and low
> Above and underground
> And in and out, and about, and about
> And round, and round, and round . . ."

It is also recorded that this chap (yclept Sir Guy the Seeker) was aided and abetted in his particular piece of tomfoolery by a 'ghastly wight' (because it rhymed with 'Sir Knight! Sir Knight!'). Now, I don't know how *you* feel about this type of medieval pop-song but personally if there's one thing I wouldn't touch with the end of an old loofah it's some ghastly wight leading me such a dance that I'm likely to bump into myself coming round the next corner. It simply isn't worth it.

Much better to proceed decorously to CRASTER, a fishing hamlet with a little harbour built by the Craster family whereon you may have to stop the car and wait while they winch a coble across the roadway. There have been Crasters in Craster since 1272, which is 37 years before the Duke of Northumberland's family arrived.

This is why we brought the 'Gaz' and the frying-pan. Because if it's between the end of May and the end of September and they've decided the herring are fat and deserving enough of being turned into the famous Craster kippers (oak-smoked and no dye added), then we can go straight to the sheds and choose a couple each to cook on the beach. It's as well to buy more than two each, actually, because improvident people who haven't brought their 'Gazes' with them are wont to sit in a semi-circle round the frying-pan looking like the Bisto Kids and slavering at the mouth rather disgustingly. Thus it is more conducive to one's own proper enjoyment and digestion to cook up a preliminary kipper or two and chuck them to the crowd, who will then proceed to run after them like famished boll weevils. The further you throw them the less likely you are to be worried again until you've licked the frying-pan and scarpered. Throw them out to sea by all means. There are some very dangerous rocks out there.

You never know—you might get a good giggle out of it as well.

The curing is done in the sheds, which are full of fish hanging on rods above the smoke while the women pack the prepared kippers into cases tacked together by the men. Meanwhile the boats, with their distinctive little tent-like awnings, bring in more herrings, crab and lobster. You can buy half a dozen Craster kippers tacked into a flat box and have them sent anywhere in the world. Most Europeans adore kippers once they've learned not to marinate them in brandy and rosemary, and serve them with *sauce Périgueux*.

Return via ALNMOUTH, taking particular note of the Foxton Development for wealthy people wishing to live in modern houses overlooking the sea and the valley of the Aln. Imagine waking here on a glorious sunny morning and considering a game of golf, or some dinghy sailing on the river. These houses have been particularly cleverly constructed, leaving the village completely unspoiled, and Alnmouth is a charming spot for those who prefer to watch, and smell, boats being built rather than tooting a tin trumpet while on holiday.

We are now leaving the coast to go inland. But before we go may I point out to you that though the total coastline of England, Wales, and Northern Ireland is 3,083 miles long only about 900 miles of it still remains completely unspoiled? If you have loved the drive down the Northumbrian coast as much as I do, then you will be interested in keeping it as it is.

Control of all development is exercised by local planning authorities and the Northumbrian authorities have done a marvellous job. There are also such bodies as the government-controlled Ministry of Land and Natural Resources, the National Parks Commission, and the Nature Conservancy. But policies change and land is subject to pressures not always in the public interest. Planning authorities only have limited funds to protect it.

The NATIONAL TRUST, founded in 1895, is not government-controlled. Probably it is the prefix 'National' which gives rise to the popular misconception, but it is in effect entirely supported by public subscription. In May 1965 a new campaign was started entitled 'Enterprise Neptune' to seek privately-owned lands which might be made over as gifts under 'inalienable ownership' to the National Trust—which land can thereafter never be sold, mortgaged, nor removed from its control excepting by will of Parliament. They are also seeking to raise £2 million to enable the Trust to buy other coastland offered for sale. Some land in Northumberland already belongs to them but not enough at present to ensure that it will remain as beautiful forever.

If you are interested in helping, write to Lawrence Rich at 'Enterprise Neptune', 42, Queen Anne's Gate, London S.W.1. He will be delighted to tell you what you can do to ensure that the coast of Northumberland remains a pleasing place to return to.

WARKWORTH comes next and here again there's a castle and also one of the only fortified bridges left in the country. It must have been awfully difficult to take *that* particular bridge with some equally determined fellow on the other end trying to stop you. This castle was once the home of the Percys and 'Harry Hotspur' was born here. Devotees of Shakespeare's Henry IV, part II, will recognise it immediately.

Warkworth is on the Coquet, the best salmon river in the North. The walks along its banks are pretty, or you might get a likely local lad to row you to the HERMITAGE, a cell in the cliffside with a tiny chapel-alcove. There are various explanations for this hermit's cave, the most sadly romantic of all being that Isabel, Lord Widdrington's daughter, tried to put her lover —Sir Bertram of Bothal (see page 51)—to the test of affection by sending him off to fight the Scots. He was badly wounded, and Isabel, regretting her foolishness, set off to nurse him back to health. On the way she was captured by a Scottish chieftain who'd always had his eye on her and who carried her off to his stronghold. Bertram promptly felt much better and departed with his brother to look for her. He seems to have lost touch with his brother *en route* because, being confronted at the walls of the chieftain's stronghold by his lady descending a ropeladder assisted by a man in Highland dress he leapt forward yelling "Vile traitor, yield that lady up" and—without giving poor Isabel a chance to explain—slew the lad (who turned out to be his brother). Isabel was also pierced to the heart while trying to retrieve the situation created by her impulsive and extremely clumsy fiancé and told the story of her capture and rescue with her dying breath. After that Bertram may have agreed with the miners on page 53 that women are bad luck. In any case it is

82

said that it was he who hewed the hermitage out of the rock and went off to live there with an effigy of his lost love for company.

Drive along the banks of the Coquet from Warkworth and cross into GUYZANCE with its lovely main street tumbling down the side of the hill amid the spring or summer flowers. To your right there's a pretty gateway leading into a perfectly delightful courtyard.

After buying fresh eggs from one of the local farms, make for the busy market town of MORPETH on what Leland called 'the Wansbeke, a praty ryver'. The family of Admiral Collingwood lived here, at Collingwood House in Oldgate Street, and the town is now a centre for everybody in the district, from miners and farmers to squires and the foxhunting fraternity.

Before returning to Newcastle you may like to make a small detour to see the absolutely fabulous, slightly crumbling pile of SEATON DELAVAL. Personally I adore this house, the finest example of Vanbrugh's work in the North of England. The 'Gay Delavals' were of Norman descent and related to William the Conqueror. What appears to have been the last entirely respectable member of the family—Admiral George Delaval—commissioned Vanbrugh in 1707. Sixteen years later the Admiral fell off his horse and perished, leaving in his wake a group of decidedly high-spirited descendants, more rakishly imbued with derring-do than even the most *louche* of their 18th-century contemporaries.

For instance, they thought it the merriest of japes to attach pulleys to the spare beds before inviting guests to stay. When their guests were asleep the pulleys would fling them through trap-doors into baths of cold water under the floorboards. When one considers the time it must have taken them to set up this particular prank one does sincerely hope the result was worth the effort.

But that wasn't all. They also had collapsible walls to the bedrooms. This, however, was apparently only because it was considered highly risible to catch people with their wigs off. It was good clean junketing, and kept the 'tweenies all agiggle! There was never anything inimical or shockingly immoral about it.

The Delavals were obviously extremely talented in the art of this, the so-popular 18th-century practical joke. They were also extremely talented at producing famous beauties of unimaginable wealth. Figure to yourself, therefore, the hopeful young blade of the day slicing himself painfully against the grain as he ponders whether to accept a weekend invitation or not. How could he guess whether somebody at this very minute was not perhaps balancing a bag of soot over the *portière* in anticipation of his delighted acceptance?

Practical jokes in these more enlightened days are considered to be cruel—but they were the fashion of that period. The house itself doesn't look a bit unkind. It looks a place where everybody was always happy.

What a *pity* there aren't any Delavals left.

Part Two

COUNTY DURHAM

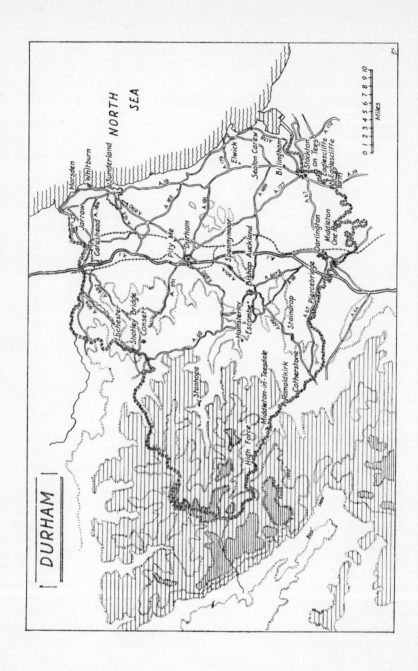

DURHAM

NORTH SEA

Marsden
Whitburn
Sunderland
Jarrow
Gateshead
A 184
A 694
A 692
Ebchester
Shotley Bridge
Consett
Stanhope
High Force
Middleton-in-Teesdale
Hamsterley
Escomb
Romaldkirk
Cotherstone
Staindrop
Piercebridge
Pity Me
Durham
Spennymoor
Bishop Auckland
Darlington
Middleton One Row
Elwick
Seaton Carew
Billingham
Stockton on Tees
Eaglescliffe
Eaglescliffe
Yarm

A 19
A 167
A 181
A 690
A 691
A 1
A 689
A 688
A 67
A 68
A 167
A 177
A 67
A 66
A 179
A 19
A 66
A 172

0 1 2 3 4 5 6 7 8 9 10
Miles

County Durham

I suppose that it is within the limits of possibility to forgive the Londoner for supposing County Durham to be in Ireland? After all, alone among English counties it is thus designated Irish fashion. In fact I've never actually heard anybody in the North-East call the county anything but 'Durham' and this is apt to baffle the visitor a little. He always thought Durham was the city called Durham which had Durham cathedral in it. Which it is.

County Durham is roughly triangular in shape and is 21st in point of size compared with other English counties. It also was once a county Palatine—a place considered not to be a county at all but a 'Bishopric'. A Prince-Bishop ruled over Durham City, Bishop Auckland, Bishop Middleham, Sadberge and Stockton, whose spiritual territory reached from Tweed to Tees and whose temporal lands reached from Tees to Tyne. Within these limits the King's Writ did not run and the Prince-Bishop exercised regal sway. He had his own courts of law, his own system of finance, his own coinage, his own troops and his own ships. This form of government survived, in attenuated state, until 1836 when the Palatinate was finally annexed to the Crown. Nevertheless, even today the monarch is also Earl Palatine of Durham.

Apart from this, the history of County Durham is very much part of that of Northumberland. When the Danes descended on Northumbria in 875 the body of St Cuthbert was moved to Chester-le-Street and, after the 995 raid, to Durham City itself. Thus the seed of the Palatinate was sown and finally King Canute, who came to slay and plunder, made his penitential journey to pay homage to St Cuthbert, completing the process of pagan conversion.

County Durham abounds in a wealth of folk-lore and superstition. The great authority on these—Mr Robert Wood—told me so much about them in half an hour that he almost put me off writing a book at all. My own painfully acquired knowledge paled in comparison and I felt I was making a rude and vainglorious attempt to say absolutely nothing of any interest to anybody. If you go to Hartlepool, and I hope you do, then firstly don't forget to ask them, "who hung the monkey?" and then to look for Mr Robert Wood.

Another delightful thing about County Durham is that it connects itself with Lewis Carroll and Alice. Lewis Carroll (Charles Lutwidge Dodgson) was the only son of the Rector of Croft and had an unknown number of sisters towards whom he displayed extreme formality, signing his letters to them "Yours sincerely".

To the Londoner, tired of attempting to quaff a quiet beer in a London pub without being faced with the information that Dickens sat, stood, slept, ate, or fell here, Alice is a charming change. Alice comes naturally, like the Roman Wall. Carpenters here, if they wear any headgear at all, stick to flat 'ats. And nobody encourages anybody to sell horrible half-crown walruses outside the Sunderland Football Ground on Saturdays.

Had Dickens really sat, stood, slept, eaten, or fallen in all the pubs in which he is reputed to have sat, stood, slept, eaten, or fallen he would in any case have had to spend his entire life running and jumping from one to the other day after day after day. And his nights fighting pachyderms.

I think, if I were lucky enough to live up North, I would live in County Durham. It is just as beautiful as Northumberland and just as kindly. And it takes not the very slightest notice of the North-South battle for supremacy going on over its head. It gets quietly on with its own business, fatly aware that, whoever wins, County Durham isn't going to lose.

Durham City

When I, as a writer, go all lyrical, then I am entirely certain to receive next morning 20 telephone calls complaining, "Dammit you've gone all lyrical."

Yet to write about DURHAM without going all lyrical is extremely difficult. First sight of the cathedral set high on its cliffside, looped by the peaty-brown River Wear can only be described as breathtaking. It is the finest example of early Norman architecture in England, the ultimate shrine of St Cuthbert, whose body was said to show no signs of decay two hundred years after he died. The tomb of the Venerable Bede is also enshrined in this cathedral, which, at first sight, has the same brooding magnificence as Chateauneuf-du-Pape.

Two booklets written by C. J. Stranks, Archdeacon of Auckland and Canon of Durham, are on sale in the entrance. They describe the lives of St Cuthbert and Bede and are fine to study since the history of County Durham is much bound up with the stories of these saints.

I don't know about Durham during the tourist season but in early May I had it to myself. The locals had all gone home to lunch and the university was on holiday. This must be the best time of year to see it, when it is utterly peaceful and with its surrounding hills spring-lambed in the sunshine. I crossed Elvet Bridge and walked up the steep, cobbled, one-vehicle lane towards the cathedral. This leads up to the North Bailey —another world, remote and studious, behind the castle which was founded by the Conqueror and surrendered by Bishop Van Mildert in 1836 for the purpose of founding a university.

The street is bounded on its other side by the most beautiful row of houses I have ever seen, mostly university buildings, each one different—particularly in the matter of doors and heavy doorknockers.

The buildings are painted pink, blue, grey, green, black, yellow; seeming to retain a rustle of silk, a decorous pantalette. At the end of the lane comes another unexpected sight. Suddenly laid out below you as you walk unwarned through an archway is the river again, running at the bottom of a wooded hillside thick with moss and starred with daffodils. As I stood there stunned with delight a fisherman came walking up towards me. "Salmon's coom back," he observed waving his trout-rod at the river.

"Did they *go*?" I asked.

"Yes," he replied. "Sign of decadent civilisation when salmon leave. Return means sign of things putting themselves in order." He waved again in the direction of the Wear. "They've coom back now," he stated with evident satisfaction. I was glad too. I felt that a salmon had just as much of a hope of 'putting things in order' as had Mr George Brown. In addition I had been puzzling for months, wondering what it was Mr George Brown reminded me of. Now—to my complete satisfaction—I suddenly knew.

You will, of course, visit the cathedral. You will see the sanctuary knocker, and Bishop Hatfield's enormous throne, pinnacled and canopied, proving better than anything else the regal sway and power held by the past Bishops of Durham.

You may also like to look for a faint cross in the floor near the North-West door. St Cuthbert held the sensible North-Country view that women should be kept in their places, though in his case he took it to the extremes of misogyny. This is odd for a saint and there are various reasons put forward for it. It has been suggested that it arose from a false charge of seduction brought against him by the daughter of a Pictish king. Others think it arose from the immoral conduct of the monks and nuns at Coldingham but, as J. E. Morris says in his 'Companion into Durham', why blame the women rather than the men? Being a woman myself, though, I think possibly Mr J. E. Morris is being a little too innocently charitable. (A thoroughly masculine trait but a dangerous one.) In any case, if a woman approached too near the tomb of St Cuthbert his body 'became troubled' and the cross on the floor marks the spot beyond which no feminine foot was once allowed to tread. This seems to have gone to the heads of some ladies who, with typical female curiosity, got up to all types of disastrous tricks in order to flaunt the edict.

Having looked at the cathedral and the castle (which is only open on weekdays) make your way to the market place to see the policeman directing the traffic by television from a little hut in the middle of the road. What surprises me is that anybody ever notices him as they drive round the corner, since he appears to be called 'CATHEDRAL' rather than 'POLICEMAN'. Nor can I imagine why this is the only spot in Britain, so far as I know, where this extremely efficient method of traffic control is used.

I was looking for Durham Gaol. One imagines it sticking starkly up high in the distance and I felt I ought at least to see this famous top-security, fearsome, gruesome stronghold. People kept giving me directions and I walked and walked, looking up at the surrounding hills. Finally I passed the charming ROYAL COUNTY HOTEL in Old Elvet and wandered up to the top of the street admiring the lovely houses. It was getting late. A man came down the street towards me. I tried again. "Could you tell me where Durham Gaol is?"

He looked surprised. "Ye're *in* it," he said.

Well, *there* it is! Standing quite prettily in a wide courtyard and the studded green doors don't even fit very well. You can see right through them.

I was reminded of the story of my friend Bill Sykes of Tyne-Tees Television, who arrived late after the rest of the unit had gone in to make a documentary. He banged on the door, a little flap opened, and a warder looked out. "Yes?" asked the warder politely. Bill explained why it was necessary for him to gain admission to the gaol immediately.

"Yes?" said the warder, "Your name please?"

"Bill Sykes," said Bill Sykes.

He got in eventually but it wasn't easy. It's difficult enough to get into Durham Gaol—your crime has to be pretty heinous —without trying to be funny with a warder into the bargain.

To one side of the gaol is Charrington's COURT INN, which is reputed to be packed with merry warders and jovial prison padres. There is also apparently some specially good beer kept in the cellar which the landlord will fetch up if you ask for it. But, as we have already pointed out, ladies on their own are definitely discouraged from going into pubs up North ("One is a pound and two is a party y'see," explained a young man to me somewhat mysteriously) and I felt that to penetrate alone into a pub which was also reputed to be packed with merry warders and jovial prison padres was more than even I—conscientious though I am—could face in pursuit of knowledge.

So I went to see the famous and very lovely Ove Arup bridge ordered by the university to link two groups of college buildings on opposite banks of the River Wear, and which won a Class I Civic Trust Award in 1965.

What a challenge *that* must have been! What nightmares of upraised hands and pre-stressed cries of "Vandalism!" the designer must have had to face as he considered his problem. The tyro blessed with no more knowledge of architecture than I might like to get a copy of the 'Northern Architect' for March 1966 in order to understand how Arup managed with only about £35,000 to design this miracle of grace—uncompromisingly 20th century though it be—which enhances rather than detracts from the beauty of the old city. And all under the watchful eyes of the church, the university, the City and County of Durham, and the Royal Fine Art Commission to boot.

When one *thinks* what the Church Commissioners have allowed to happen to the once-lovely vista of St Paul's from Ludgate Circus . . .

From here I went to FINCHALE PRIORY, which I approached by means of a very long, hot walk from the bus stop halfway to Chester-le-Street. The Priory stands at the bottom of a steep hillside in another loop of the river Wear and to my horror the first thing I saw through its graceful archways was a hideous caravan site. Most unusual for either Northumberland or County Durham. I wonder how on earth it was ever allowed to get there.

H.M. Stationery Office have printed a 6d pamphlet about the Priory and a decidedly cleaned-up life story of St Godric, the hermit who first made his home there in 1110, amid the poisonous snakes. St Godric is more popularly supposed to have been 'as selfish and dirty an old anchorite as ever attained the brevet rank of sainthood'. He died aged 105, after which Henry Puiset, somewhat startlingly described (though not by H.M. Stationery Office) as the 'eldest illegitimate son of Bishop Puiset', endowed it as a Benedictine cell to Durham. There is a plan of the ruins on the cover of the pamphlet which is absolutely useless since it does not include the river. It tells you where North and South are but, without benefit of a compass tucked in one's handbag, this helps not in the slightest. So I went into the cyclist's café where hot or cold chocolate or chicken soup are dispensed from a vending machine, and asked for a pot of tea. The proprietress was absolutely charming and handed me her own mug marked 'Anne' and decorated with squirrels, enjoining me merely not to break it. She also made me some tea.

Sensing that I was weary and somewhat disenchanted with Finchale Priory she tried to be helpful about buses. "They don't run very often," she said. "You'd best make for the 4.20 now. You catch it at the bus stop just by the bare patch."

Luckily I reached the top of the hill at 4.10 because there was no Stop-sign and there were three bare patches. So I went to the village shop a little way down the road. "Where's the bus stop?" I asked.

"Why, it's joost be the paatch!" replied the shopkeeper. So I went back to the three patches and picked the middle one. After about half an hour's wait all the cars were drawing away and night was drawing on. I asked one or two car-drivers who replied they didn't think a bus came along here at all. Suddenly an old lady appeared, trotting merrily along the road with a basketful of cooking apples in one hand and a crooked stick in the other. She smiled at me as she advanced. "Waayting for the Chester boos?" she asked. "It's joost yon . . . look" pointing into the middle distance.

"Will it stop?" I asked.

"Stop?" cried the old lady. "Eh *no* Pet! Noooo!"

I looked at her in despair. "But I was told this was the bus stop!" I moaned piteously.

"Eddn't no boos stops in t'coontry," she replied. "Leastways —eddn't if'n you doan't stop 'em, see?" She turned as the bus rounded the corner and waved an imperious stick. The bus stopped immediately. She smiled at me again. "Layke thaat see?"

she said. "Tata then, Pet!" and went trotting up the road again. I waved my thanks as I sailed past and she waved her stick once more.

The trip back to Chester-le-Street, where you pick up the Newcastle connection, costs only 10d and the views are marvellous. But don't forget that if you're in t'coontry eddn't no boos stops if'n you doan't stop 'em.

See?

Hartlepool

I have said if I had the luck to live in the North-East I would live in County Durham. Well, if I had the luck to live in County Durham I would live near Hartlepool. If I had the luck.

This seems to surprise people. I wonder why. Supposing you could choose where you would like to live what would you look for? Incredible beauty? Hartlepool certainly hasn't got that, but incredible beauty is usually untouchable and people living in its midst seldom ever notice it in any case.

Friendliness? I found more friendliness in Hartlepool than anywhere else in the North-East. It is a town big enough not to be nosey yet small enough to ensure you don't fall ill alone and die without anybody noticing you didn't take the milk in.

Shopping facilities? Like most of the larger towns in County Durham, Hartlepool has knocked down and cleared away its rubble. A large shopping precinct is being built and there are already some nice little fashion boutiques for the purveyance of p.v.c. and mini-skirts.

A place for dining-out in style? I had two of the best lunches of my stay in the North-East at the GRAND—a surprisingly chic hotel packed with surprisingly chic ladies and gents eating surprisingly chic meals in the restaurant under the benevolent aegis of Norman, the maître d'hôtel.

Sports, cultural activities? All the personnel at the Town Hall are friendly and highly available. The Industrial Development Officer, Mr Brian Belshaw, will hand you a Directory of Organisations and will see that you are invited to the Mayoress's teaparties to meet other newcomers. Mayors and Mayoresses in

95

the North-East do not behave as if they had suddenly achieved supernatural unction, separating them forever from their paltry fellowmen. They work hard and, as last year's Mayor—Alderman Rennie Warnes—told me when I had tea with him in the Mayor's Parlour: "We're dealing with people, not institutions here. We have time to stop and talk and listen to any little personal problems we might be able to solve."

The *Northern Daily Mail* is Hartlepool's own newspaper. Reporters are constantly looking for copy and so everything comes to light. About 130,000 people are reading their local paper every day. It might be much better for the London boroughs if we all read ours. Then we'd know what was going on too and our local Mayors might have to be as helpful and charming as was Alderman Warnes.

As for sport, there's everything from golf to skin-diving, but the saltiest sport of the lot is to become a member of the Hartlepool Sailing Club, in which I spent too short an evening as the guest of 'Tot' Richardson, the Commodore. The sailing here is sea-sailing. Hartlepool spreads into SEATON CAREW, which can't be called staggeringly beautiful either. But neither can you ride (or walk) 2 miles along the sand-dunes of the South coast without meeting anybody else, like you can in Seaton.

I met Tot at my favourite pub, the MACORVILLE, in my favourite village, ELWICK, which is ten minutes by car outside Hartlepool, a drive on which you are unlikely to encounter much apart from a beautiful high-trotting pony proudly pulling a delicate little carriage.

"But!" they cry. "We have much *much* prettier villages in the North-East!"

Yes, indeed you have. But you see, Elwick spilling down the hillside under its chestnut trees was the first pretty village I saw when I was still a raw Southerner looking for a pit-heap. And the MacOrville has Thora Warrand's super fresh turkey sandwiches and Ronnie Warrand's fruit-salad-type Pimm's. It has Mr Warrand père's "Hul-LO! I remember *you*! Ee yes! You've come back to see me, Hinny!" And tales of the Women's Institute getting sloshed by mistake at a home-made-wine tasting.

"You need a knife and fork to drink our potato wine! And home-made beer! You have to wait for it to ooze out of the

Durham Cathedral

Barnard Castle and the
River Tees

The High Street, Stockton-on-Tees

High Force

bottle and then you can chew it for hours. It's not made of fish-stock, you know!"

"We have real fresh flowers in here all the year round. None of your plastic. And none of them tourist buses. We can't be doing with them."

"Do you know, Pet, that, in the old days, if you swore they fined you 3d, if you called a man a rogue they fined you 6d, if you hit him they fined you 1/-. But if you called him a Scotsman they fined you 6/8d!"

"They grow trees in the South, Hinny. But they grow men in the North."

All this takes place to the click of dominoes. And possibly one of the players might be local artist and chemist Mr R. W. Johnson, who claims to have Alice's personal photograph album in his cottage, with a picture of Lewis Carroll in it; and one of her dog, who had tusks like the walrus; and one of her parents' gardener, who wore a little hat like the carpenter. When I went back to see it I couldn't find Mr Johnson. But *you* might.

So if I had the luck to live in the North-East in County Durham near Hartlepool I would live in Elwick. In North Close where they've built a modern development amid the old houses in the grounds of Elwick Hall and where the value of a large, new, detached house is leaping up monthly but might possibly still be obtained for £4,000.

To return to Hartlepool (to which I sincerely hope you are not still adding the prefix 'West'). In spite of its new-found modernity it still retains, and I hope always will retain, the atmosphere of what it once was—a prosperous Victorian sea-side town. The ghosts of little girls going uncomfortably to the beach in crinolines and starched pinafores hang around the square and it is quite a disappointment not to see beach-huts on wheels at Seaton Carew. It was created by Ralph Ward Jackson, a Stockton-born ex-solicitor who built there a port of his own to avoid competition when shipping coal. When he put his Port Bill before Parliament the opposition was great, but just prior to the day of the final reading there was a terrible tempest and 8 vessels were wrecked on the shore while trying to get into Hartlepool.

The 8 masters declared that their ships had foundered where Jackson intended to build his port and that this harbour would have saved them. And so the Bill was approved. This port is now being used as a base for the North Sea Oil Exploration campaign.

At the top of Church Street is the statue of Ralph Ward Jackson, his back turned firmly upon Christ Church which was built in his time and with the vicar of which he once became so highly incensed that he had the entrance to the church bricked up in order to stop him conducting his Sunday services.

Early history tells of Northumbria's first Nun, St Heiu, who in 640, under the auspices of St Aidan, established a monastery on the rock where St Hilda's Parish Church now stands. In 649 St Hilda took charge of the monastery but 8 years later she moved to Whitby where she established the famous Abbey. The original monastery was destroyed by the Vikings in 800. In 1066 William the Conqueror brought with him to England Robert de Brus, whose son married the daughter of the lord of the manor of Hart. This started a connection with Hartlepool which lasted until Robert Bruce VIII was exiled in 1306 for claiming the Scottish crown. It is generally believed that Robert Bruce IV planned the present St Hilda's in 1190 and his tomb, much weatherbeaten after lying in the open for nearly 2 centuries, now occupies the de Brus chapel. The church is still somehow redolent of wooden ships and sail, tarred rope, and terrible storms at sea.

From here you can go down to the Fish Quay and see the fish being unloaded and sold at 8.0 a.m. You might catch Thora Warrand drinking strong tea and eating bacon-and-eggs in the little café nearby. In addition to the 'MacOrville' the Warrands have a fish-game-and-poultry business, which accounts for the succulence of her turkey sandwiches. The Harbour Master is Captain McLean, who'll tell you how snow seldom settles in Hartlepool and there's never any fog. There is sometimes something called a 'sea-fret' which is *such* a pretty cognomination for the gentle mist occasionally floating harmlessly in-shore. Or you might meet Doug the foyboatman, one of the self-employed workers who go out in little boats to take ropes from the ships and tie them to the bollards.

"You go under the bow and get the rope and put it on the buoy and go under the stern for the stern rope. Head rope and stern rope, y'see? And it's touchy whether your boat sinks, y'see? But we've had motorboats for two years. Used to be done with one oar in the stern of the rowing-boat, y'see?"

Or you might walk along the old Town Wall by the entrance to the Old Fish Sands where the merchants used to come and buy the fish straight off the cobles. This is now more of a perfect sun-trap than an old fish sand. Or go to the Gray Art Gallery and Museum, particularly in order to admire the truly evocative conservatory with real *plashing* fountain and the musty perfume of long-gone lovers plighting a variety of troths behind the *nephrolepis exaltata*. The paintings here are more atmospheric than expert but the portraits of healthy pink-cheeked past councillors are indicative of the excellent tonic properties of a sea-fret or two.

Harry Carter, once Keeper of the Lighthouse and now verger of St Hilda's, is another robust advertisement for Hartlepool. He's 73 and not a grey hair on his well-endowed scalp. His daughter, Avis, was a film-star and he has two handsome sons. The oldest inhabitant of the town is a relative of his, George Brown, aged 101.

Harry will tell you how to go out for 'runnydowns' (baitworms) after the dredgers have deepened the channel and how Avis still makes her own bread though she's married now to a film executive. And how he once went in the *Medway Queen* from Southend to Margate to see the conical buoys which are 'a lighthouse-keeper's dream'. And how he stopped smoking when he caught himself taking a drag behind a pillar at St Hilda's during the sermon.

"I'm not what you would call a Biblical man though I have learned in whatsoever state I am therewith to be content. I heard that in 1915 and I've rememberd it ever since. Philippians IV: 11. I used to keep the Bible with a little bit of paper stuck in it in the lighthouse. Chick Henderson was in our choir, y'know. Nobody could sing 'Begin the Beguine' like him. I used to play the flute. I don't like pop-music. It isn't elevating . . ."

As I left Harry Carter he saw me to the door of his house and said something which still puzzles me a little. "Well, goodbye!" he said "I hope I'm pleased to meet you!"

Well! I hope he is too.

Sunderland

I went to SUNDERLAND three times and I could have done with more. For instance, you cannot possibly look lost in Sunderland. Some anxious citizen will always ask you: "Where're ye gang then, Pet?"

Well-born London ladies carefully trained to reply, "What the hell has it go to do with *you*?" to men asking this particular question should give themselves pause. It is more than probable, as happened to me, that the man asking the question has halted his step on noticing another man 500 yards up the road pointing out a direction. He has therefore waited to make sure you understood the direction given you by the first man. (In my case I didn't. But then I never do.)

I started with Mr J. Bridge, Director of Education ("47 new schools since the war, oldest-established child-guidance clinic, and largest regional Technical College in the country outside London") who insisted on walking with me through the town —and a surprisingly large, clean, modern town it is—to the office of Mr J. T. Shaw, the Director of Public Libraries and of the Museum and Art Gallery. "It's only round the corner," said Mr Bridge as I protested that I didn't want to waste his time, "but you might get lost". It wasn't just round the corner, it was quite a walk. But he was quite right about my getting lost.

Mr Shaw spent ages taking me round what must be one of the most modern and beautifully laid out museums in the country. Here the most interesting exhibits are of Sunderland glass and pottery.

Look for goblets fashioned as pathetic little memorials to pit disasters ("183 children killed"), glass rolling pins pre-prandially inscribed "Lover's Gift", pink lustre Sunderland pottery, highly ornate monks' chamber-pots (". . . *there* you are Myfanwy. Didn't I tell you? . . ."), "Sailor's Farewell" mugs with a ship (his) a little cottage (hers) and the giver's own verse painted on them. It would be well to invest in 'The Potteries of Sunderland and District' written by Mr Shaw himself and on sale in the museum (3/6d) because this particular museum is one in which it would be a pity to miss anything. I would merely add that the oil paintings are extremely interesting and particularly well restored.

The building also houses a library which is spanking new and entirely modern in design, an object of envy for anybody as addicted to libraries as I am.

Mr. Shaw disagrees with Mr Johnson of Elwick (see page 97) upon the subject of the Walrus and the Carpenter. There's a very stuffed walrus indeed in the museum which used to be in the old museum and is supposed to have inspired Lewis Carroll, and "ships' carpenters used to wear little hats just like Tenniel's carpenter's hat," says Mr Shaw.

For lunch in Sunderland I can highly recommend the ubiquitous Binns' GAY TRAY & BEARPIT which is crowded at 12.30 p.m. and almost empty by 1.0 because the North begins and ends work earlier. Soup, eggburger, chips, and coffee 4/4d. For a posher spread the GRAND (deliciously old-world) provides a 3-course luncheon for 11/- (dinner 13/-) and Sunderland also possesses a salutary lesson to all British railway buffets, clean, fresh, comfortable and well-serviced.

I went from there to what I thought was the bus stop. It wasn't the bus stop and as I stood bewildered a man came up to me and said, "Uh-uh Hen I see you're pouting." When I explained exactly why I was 'pouting' he took me to the bus stop and told me all about being an ex-tram-driver. He joined me on the bus, "Nothing else to do just now anyway, Hen," and put me off at the right stop for Doxford's. This is off Trimdon Street right in the dock area, which one would expect to be extremely ugly. It isn't. You get a fabulous view over the Wear of ships, factories and cranes in a setting of rose-pink with green fields fading away into the distance behind them.

I suppose everybody knows what Doxford's is—it is now The

Doxford and Sunderland Shipbuilding and Engineering Company. The offices all run off a lovely old Victorian Hall like a Paxton miniature palace with a wrought-iron staircase, galleries, glass dome, model ships, aspidistras, old photographs. Proudly in the middle stands a working model of the 'North Sands' engine, which in reality is as large as a 2-storey house, and (for the benefit of my male readers) is a 9 cylinder opposed piston 2-stroke oil engine, with cylinder bores of 760 mm. and a combined stroke of 2,180 metres which develops 21,000 B.H.P. at 119 r.p.m.: it measures about 60 feet long, 13 feet wide and 34 feet high and weighs 655 tons. The Doxford Engine is the only British-designed large marine oil engine and in the case of the 'North Sands' is controlled by the Captain from the bridge. Personally I haven't the slightest idea what it *does*. I only know that it is very beautiful. If you should want to see it, and visit the shipbuilding and engineering works, write to the Works Manager and ask to be included in a party.

The other thing to see in Sunderland is the Jobling factory where they make Pyrex. The glass-blowing department is a cross between the Royal Mint and Dante's Inferno. There's a hot oven in the middle shuddering with rage and all round it are collected shadowy figures of men gathering blobs of molten glass on long pipes, twirling, swinging, blowing, moulding, and steaming. In the forefront of this company of craftsmen stands a tall fellow with cheeks blown out to impossible enormity. You are convinced that this poor chap, once he stops all this blowing, will end with a face collapsed like a bloodhound's. But he doesn't. His extended chops spring back into shape like new elastic and you know that his children and grandchildren always had the best balloons in Sunderland and that South African *biltong* tastes to him like the tenderest steak.

Bryan Simpson, aged 22 and just married, took me round and explained it all to me. Then he took me back on the bus, paid my fare, and pointed out that Sunderland is only 4 hours from Central London anyway. He said he felt sorry for people who didn't have the sea and countryside at their doorstep and a nice little bungalow like his to live in. I remembered that the other day it took me an hour and 10 minutes to get from Richmond to Sloane Square and agreed with him.

While in Sunderland you should also visit The Civic Theatre;

St Peter's Church at MONKWEARMOUTH, and the lovely little seaside village of WHITBURN, by comparison with which Rottingdean appears frankly meretricious, are also well worth a visit.

The Civic Theatre, which is probably only known to most of us because it's where P. J. Proby split his pants, has an interesting history which was explained to me by the Director, Mr Reggie Birks. Some time ago Moss Empires gave up this theatre and it started to go downhill. When closing was suggested, the local Council decided that they wanted to give the younger generation something they themselves had never had—a chance to see good theatre, opera, ballet, and to hear music played by the famous people they had hitherto only heard about. So they put 6d on the rates and started the first true Civic Theatre in Britain.

"The rebirth of the theatre will come through young people," Mr Birks told me. "Forty to fifty thousand come here every year from all over the North-East and they don't come just to hold hands in the back rows. The corporation insist that the programmes must be of the best possible quality. We do have the Beatles. They came twice and the first time they were third on the Bill. But we also have poetry, pantomime, Sadler's Wells, the Royal Shakespeare Company, Ballet Rambert and the Royal Ballet.

"A good many people still think that the theatre is chiefly provided as an intellectual social pastime for an eccentric minority, or as some people put it 'the enlightened'. This is to some extent true, the result of the policy of commercial managements who have produced and still are producing for a certain section of the privileged public on their traditionally established number 1 circuits, ignoring vast areas all over Great Britain that have never had an opportunity of seeing good theatre unless they could afford to travel long distances, and it is the people who cannot afford to do this we need to contact. If it is lack of a suitable theatre, then today this is the local authorities' responsibility. If our theatres are to remain—be appreciated—flourish —we must quickly overthrow this 'highbrow special set' complex and do our utmost to have theatre arts generally accepted as a vital and essential part of our communal leisure, cultural and educational existence, as are schools, libraries, museums, and art galleries. Civic Theatre, to be a success, must be a social service.

"We get financial help from firms like Jobling's who realise it is good for their labour problem to have a healthy Civic Theatre. They have them in Belgium, you know. You don't see the Belgian younger generation having to be forced to go to a concert, do you?"

Actually you don't. I *am* three-quarters Belgian and so I know.

"We're very arts-minded up here anyway. Much more so than in the South. Irving made his debut in Sunderland, you know! And then take the way we all go on about the young being no good. Skiffle was their own beat—they invented it. And *we* took it and commercialised it. Then we have the audacity to blame them for what happened to it!"

Mr Birks is enthusiastic, sympathetic and far-sighted. Civic Theatres are his greatest abiding interest. Joblings may realise it is good for their labour problem to have a Civic Theatre. But it's also awfully good for the Sunderland Civic Theatre to have Mr Birks.

St Peter's Church is within walking distance of the centre of Sunderland and was founded by Benedict Biscop in 674 on land granted to him by King Ecgfrith for the establishment of a monastery. To this monastery came a little boy of 7 named Bede who was destined to make the North-East corner of England a centre of light and learning and incidentally to tell us most of what we now know about the history of this period. The present vicar will unlock the church and explain points of interest to visitors, and the little booklet, 'St Peter's Church, Monkwearmouth', costing 1/-, is excellent for the history and descriptions contained in it. The West Wall in particular is still the original and is one of the only remaining relics of the monastery's Saxon days.

Whitburn is a peaceful village best seen at dusk with the white houses glimmering around the village green and a wonderful view of the sea and the lights of Sunderland from the quiet churchyard. Children's voices call from a long way away, birds stir and twitter a little, and there's a lovely walk back to the shore through a wicket-gate and over the fields.

Should it appear that the last pages have been too elevating you can always round off the evening by visiting the SEABURN HOTEL which is only just up the road from Whitburn. It is run by Mr & Mrs Forrest, who appear successfully able to separate the noisy young in their Moonlight Bar discothèque—gnashing upon their 'Tall in the Saddle' hamburgers (3/-) or 'Neptune's Supper' Whitburn Bay haddock (4/6d, and just fractionally cannibalistic, one feels, of Neptune)—from their parents dining sedately in the restaurant for around 10/6d on which is known as a 'Discothèque Supper' but isn't as frenetic as it sounds.

Or one can carry on to South Shields.

South Shields

Having admired the lights of SOUTH SHIELDS from North Shields at night (see page 47) it is interesting to visit the place itself by day since there are one or two matters here of historical interest.

There is the lifeboat memorial to William Wouldhave, the story of which is recounted on page 145. The original model of the first lifeboat is in the Central Library and Museum.

The remains of ARBEIA, the Roman Fort, are on view in the Roman Park on the Lawe, which in Roman times seems to have been an island between the two mouths of the river Tyne. These remains comprise a Headquarters building, ten storehouses, and the defences of a Roman army stores base for seaborne supplies to provide the needs of an expeditionary force maintained by coastwise shipping in the Emperor Severus's campaigns against the Caledonians and Maetae early in the 3rd century. On the site is a museum housing the unique and world-famous Regina tombstone which Barates of Pamlyra set up in memory of his British wife, and the equally well-known Victor tombstone set up by Numerianus in memory of his former slave, Victor the Moor. The sword displayed in the museum is the first known example of pattern welding, and the collection of gold and silver coins extend from Nero to Commodus.

So far as sightseeing is concerned, I would point out that the Planetarium in South Shields is one of the very few in Britain outside London. And to those of my readers courageous enough to drag caravans behind them over the winding roads of England I would add that South Shields is an excellent spot in which to rest them, since it is not only a good seaside resort with sandy beaches but also a convenient point from which to visit the surrounding places of beauty and interest.

The caravan sites are open to all authorised caravanners from Easter to October at 4/- per day or 25/- weekly.

The MARINE GROTTO is a place of interest at MARSDEN, though —to me—the approach to it, 90 feet down the side of a cliff, suspended in a little lift one can see through the bottom of, is absolutely appalling. The restaurant, which is well run by the Vaux Breweries, is hewn out of a cave in the side of a rock which was once occupied by Peter the Hermit. Peter was the eloquent French monk, the main instrument of the agitation which brought about the first Crusade, and this, though on a smaller scale, was his 11th-century dwelling. Lunch, tea, or dinner are served in the Marine Grotto, and H.P., ketchup and mustard. Somebody called 'Mars the Pirate' used to sleep, apparently completely sober, in the cocktail bar when the place was a smugglers' haunt. This bar now sports fish-tanks full of particularly fierce moustachioed piscatorial specimen. The beach below is wide and attractive, backed with cliffs and caves, and a popular summer resort.

It may have been the strain of having to face the dreaded lift journey upwards again which caused me to go and stand once more at the wrong bus stop. But this never seems to matter anywhere in the North-East. Somebody always comes along to rescue one.

This time a jolly old body on her way home with the shopping took an interest in me. "Boos here don't coom for a while," she stated, "Are you gang to Soonderland?" When I said that actually I was going the other way the smile left her face and she lifted her arms in alarm and dismay. "Eeeee Pet, you're at the wrong boos! Eeeee—how terrible *that* is for you, isn't it now?"

I agreed that it was indeed. So she went straight back with me in the direction from which she'd just walked to accompany me to the right stop. And waited with me until the bus arrived just to make sure I remembered to board it.

"Gang to the football?" she enquired.

Which is how I went to my first football match.

The Soccer Thing

They're very *keen*—one might almost say *exalté*—about football up here. So much so that many females living in the South with lawn-mowing gentlemen are deeply afraid that if they move to the North-East their husbands will remain permanently at football matches when they're not watching pretty dollies taking all their clothes off in Working Men's Clubs.

I decided that possibly the more passionate of these females might join their husbands both in sport and strip and never mind about the lawn. Sunderland were playing Chelsea at Roker Park, and Chelsea being my own home town this seemed a rather splendid opportunity for finding out whether football was a game the little woman was ever likely to understand.

It isn't.

To reach a football match you follow a lot of men going to a football match. They do not look like men going to a pub. They walk more deliberately, in pairs, and look more like men not going anywhere in particular.

"Stand with the Chelsea supporters," they warned me in Newcastle. "Otherwise you might get lynched."

"How do I find them?" I enquired.

"They'll be in blue," they told me.

They were. Only by the time I discovered them they turned out to be at the opposite end of the field, safely in their numbers and bluely unreachable in the distance.

"Stand right at the back of the covered stand," they also warned me, "or you might get knocked down." I must say the whole thing sounded appreciably appalling. Here am I—a hot-house plant if ever there was one—getting lynched and knocked down in the pursuit of happiness for a lot of foolish London ladies I am never even likely to meet.

I took up my position at the back of the covered stand, sucking a small hot-dog and hoping for the best. I gazed helplessly at a programme confidentially informing me that somebody called Kirkup played for the Hammers which immediately conjured up a hoard of vampires nipping each other in the shin, and that some 'unexpected home lapses', which sounded fractionally filthy, had prevented Tommy Docherty's side from doing something important. I noticed that Chelsea goalkeeper, Peter Bonetti, had been brilliant all season and hoped he wasn't having a relapse. And that Chelsea had been 'one of the busiest clubs in the country this year' which sounded as if they might be getting rather tired.

So far so good. James felt she knew pretty well what she was at, which was that she was at something she hadn't a hope of ever understanding if she lived to be senile. The excitement began to hot up, peanuts abounded, music blared. I felt very tired and fetched another hot-dog. And I realised that men going to football matches also wear specially reinforced boots.

That was when three strong men trod on me as I tried to get back to my place. Here am I, alone in this stand miles from the Chelsea supporters, being thoroughly disfigured before the thing has even started. Not only are my feet frozen like Macfisheries' fish-sticks but they are now also mangled. And I bet it'll hurt dreadfully when they finally come to.

The music gets louder, vintage rattles and car-hooters are produced. A lethal-looking banner is unfurled under my left ear. Four girls in red-striped boaters take up a stance in front of me and start to yell "Glorry glorry hey-hey-ha-ha-oo-oo!" in as creepy an exhibition of unfemininity as it has ever been my lot to witness. They sound like lady cannibals emitting tribal calls at breakfast. They follow this particular rendering with "Glorry glorry Sun-der-LAND," with the addition of what sounds suspiciously like "Chel-SEA pee-pee" though I can really hardly believe it. "Nothing very original about *these* calls," says the man next to me. Well . . . Heaven preserve me from an Original Call then.

Two fifty-seven p.m. and excitement has reached fever-pitch.

The music blares louder, people start pushing, and I am smothered in curly hair, old macs, and nylon-fur linings. By the time I have managed to extricate myself the players have appeared down there in their dear little clean shorts, sexy legs bouncing about the field, looking incredibly idiotic. There's a roar, an orgiastic swaying of bodies, and they're off, losing a Pools fortune for millions of hopeful humans while I extricate myself again from curly hair, old macs, and nylon-fur linings.

"Saw 'em *up*!" yells the man behind me, leaning heavily upon my head. "Groooh! Goo joomp in the laayke. Ayeh! Leave the coontry, why *doan't* ya?" The man on my left is by now pushing his right elbow into something I didn't even know I *had* until he leant on it, and screaming, "Nice ball nice ball nice BALL!" while the gentleman on my right has just dropped the entire contents of his flaming pipe into the pocket of my winter overcoat.

"Aw aw—dir*tee* dir*tee*," yell the boater-hatted Amazons in front of me and this cry is taken up. "DirTEE DirTEE," chant those around me, jumping up and down with a tenacity verging on monomania and what's left of my extremities. "Oo-aw! He's *dead*. He's givin' the ball *back*. What's *he*? The Salvation Army? Ooooo! It's bloody pa-THE-tic!"

This last speaker is punched in the back by the man behind him. He turns round suddenly, knocking me off balance, and somebody else sits on my face. I manage to avoid a flutter of tin heels and rise just as one of the players does something clever and a concerted cry of, "Ooooooh! GLORious!" drives me against the crush-bar which happens to be well in line with my pancreas. No sooner have I recovered my breath but somebody bunts me on the nose with the lethal banner. "Bloody cretin! Whose side are *you* on?" yells the banner-holder. The banner is by now inextricably mixed with my crowning glory. Suddenly he shrieks "Thut's it THUT'S IT!" raising the banner and three-quarters of my scalp. "Ooooo grotty. What a bloody way to play!"

"'E's tired of carrying two blokes on 'is back, see?" explains the man on my right. *Two* blokes on his back? Lucky old *him*! I've been carrying three-quarters of the entire covered stand on my back for the last half-hour and I've lost a good deal of my tonsure and all my breath to say nothing of my second hot-dog as well. By now I am convinced that the whole situation will get a good deal worse before it's better and I decide to leave.

Leave? Ha! The incidence of people actually wishing to leave football matches in the North-East is so small as to be entirely negligible. You *can't* leave.

You are poked in both eyes at once. "Oooo stupid! Shocking. Oooooo!" You are clipped sharply between the unprintables. "Oooo-ow. It's pa-THE-tic!" Your head is caught in a two-man pelvic grip. "Nice ball nice nice *nice*. OOOOO! Where're you goin' *now*, Mother's Milk?" Somebody beats you extremely forcibly ten times on the transcendental id, weeping uncontrollably. "Cretin cretin CRETIN!" Arms and legs flail wildly. Rattles, car-hooters, banners, peanuts. Red-striped boaters. Banners. More peanuts, (this time with unexpectedly sharp edges), rattles, car-hooters. Feet.

Feet.

Soccer-*schmoccer*. I don't think it's for us girls. What the hell's wrong with *you* mowing the lawn, Marion? It's a damn sight safer than *this*, let me tell you.

Darlington

Now DARLINGTON is nice. It is well-proportioned and bou-
tiqued, delightfully endowed with charming little side-lanes,
and full of interest. For instance, if you arrive by train, you will
see displayed in the rather hideous station the excellently-
preserved and obviously much-loved little 'Locomotion' all
painted like a child's Triang toy. This was the very first railway
engine in the world, the one which opened the George Stephen-
son/Edward Pease line between Stockton and Darlington in 1825.

Many people have said, "Why choose Stockton and Darlington when you could have had Manchester and Liverpool?"
(which particular line followed this one in 1830).

Well. Why *anybody* in their right mind should choose Manchester and Liverpool when they could have Stockton and
Darlington is a complete mystery to me. And it is possible that
George Stephenson/Edward Pease felt exactly as I do. After all,
it was *their* railway.

The early line was 25 miles long, cost nearly £150,000, and
was the property of only 60 canny shareholders. The 'Locomotion' cost £500 and was built in Newcastle. The chief instiga-
tors and supporters of the project (which replaced an earlier and
less revolutionary one for a canal) were the rich Darlington
Quakers. And indeed Darlington, on the river Skerne, still
retains a Victorian probity more of perfume than of sight or
sound.

Darlington, like the rest of County Durham, is about to be
redeveloped and given 'pedestrian and vehicular segregation'.
Personally I liked it as I last saw it—all Tubwell Row, Crown

Bilsdale

Whitby Harbour

Staithes

Richmond Castle

Street and Skinnergate of it. It has a superlative cattle market in the Shambles on Saturdays—not exactly the uncannily preserved, smocked-old-yokelry thing expected by the Londoner, but interesting nevertheless to those whose only annual sight of a cow is that of the embarrassed creature standing in front of the Royal Exchange being thoughtlessly milked in full sight of a curious crowd of stockbrokers.

I am not dismissing Darlington, which really is rewarding to visit, but I cannot help enthusing in particular about its truly magnificent bus-station from which it appears one can reach most of the beauties of County Durham within a very short time.

EGGLESCLIFFE, with its richly modern, well-landscaped housing development almost on the edge of the village green, summer-sleepy and rose-hung. Stop at Charrington's tiny POT & GLASS by the side of the old Norman Church and think how lovely to live here, right in the middle of the country yet within 20 minutes of Darlington, Middlesbrough, or Stockton.

One of the first railway accidents is recorded at Egglescliffe Church. In 1827 among the burials was "a stranger killed by the steam machine". It is also the fault of the railways that the village nearby is called Eaglescliffe. Some meddling little bureaucrat decided all by himself that Egglescliffe was a mis-spelling and altered the name of the junction. In fact the old English word for eagle was 'arn' as in Arncliffe; and in any case one cannot entirely blame him alone. In the 17th century some tampering little vicar or other went right back through the parish register altering 'Eggle' to 'Eagle'. Which unforgiveable piece of vandalism all goes to show that neither civil servants or ecclesiastics have *ever* had enough to do.

To return for a minute to the 'Pot & Glass' note the lovely carved bar-fronts, quite obviously once dressers since the handles and keyholes are still visible. And don't leave without trying a fresh cheese-and-raw-onion roll or—if you're foppish about raw onion—one of the really meaty pork-pies encased in marvellous pastry lacking the usual soggy-flannel inner wall. You might like to visit Egglescliffe Hall, more for its beauty than its history, and then cross the river to YARM.

The old bridge was built in 1400 by Bishop Skirlaw and embodies parts of an earlier bridge mentioned in 1305. In 1805 a new iron bridge was built at a cost of £8,000 and one arch of Bishop Skirlaw's bridge was demolished. At that moment the entire new iron bridge fell slap into the river and it is Bishop Skirlaw's bridge which is still in use today. It stands up to the stream of heavy tankers and long-distance lorries as it supported, over 550 years ago, the ox-carts of the Middle Ages.

It's a pity about the heavy tankers and long distance lorries because apart from them Yarm is a sort of cobbled British Bruges. It is essential to walk in order to appreciate the views at the top of the little side yards next to every third cottage or so. One has the impression of being in a picture-gallery. Each small glimpse is different. Here a Constable, there a Cézanne, River, trees, ivy, thatch, pantiles, deep-red brick.

The house-fronts on the main street are painted green, blue, white. Every pub looks equally inviting, leaning against the next in the imposing shade of the large OLD KETTON OX INN.

I don't know where all that heavy traffic is going, rushing and crashing through Yarm as it does. But it's a pity because this is one of the very few unpleasing modernisms to be found in the whole of the North-East.

The other absolutely super village which must be mentioned with regard to the environs of Darlington is MIDDLETON-ONE-ROW which is in fact one row of perfectly charming houses high on a hillside overlooking a curve of the river Tees and the well-tended farmland in the valley opposite. I can imagine nothing more peaceful than a stay of perhaps just a weekend at the DEVONPORT HOTEL there, most excellently run and luxuriously and delightfully decorated, situated right in the centre of the one row of perfectly charming houses aforementioned.

Let my readers not imagine that the foregoing is all that is of beauty and interest around Darlington. As we go round County Durham in the next few pages it might be well to remember that whereas I have already said that Northumberland is the fifth largest county in England I have also mentioned the fact that County Durham is the twenty-first. Which makes it smallish. Let us understand therefore that what is easily reachable from Darlington is also very near most other places in the county.

Stockton

Stockton is yet another pleasant surprise for the Londoner.
Particularly on market days (Wednesday and Saturday) when
the pubs are open all day and stalls are set up for about half a
mile on each side of the old Town Hall, built in 1735, and in the
middle of the widest high street in Europe.

Men, women (wearing velvet go-to-market toques), children,
dogs, pies, fish, biscuits, sweaters, cakes, prams, bright purple
nighties, piles of eiderdowns. Huge fresh mushrooms 4/- a
pound, tiny sweet Guernsey tomatoes, oranges, rhubarb, green
rubber gloves. Surely she's not *really* thinking of doing the
whole sitting-room in apple-blossom cotton on such a rich blue
background?

From the back, the covered stalls look hilariously like stout
ladies with slipped petticoats. "Three pairs, *any* size, 'arf a
crown!" but you fail to push your way through the crowd to
find out what the undoubted bargain is. Elastic remnants hang
over the edges of old cardboard boxes mixed with bathing suits
and Butter Puffs. "What is the delicious secret of a Marsh &
Baxter Pork Pie?"

"Good morning," says a lady in a bright yellow jacket, stopping to chat, "though I doan't know what's good about it." The
Town Hall clock emits muffled, tuneless bangs like a man walking through mashed potatoes.

In the covered Shambles, skinned rabbits lie pitifully, inde-
cently splayed out on their backs. A nun buys one red apple
and rubs it on her sleeve. I try an egg-and-bacon open pie which
is simply delicious, and I wonder why you never see any plain

carpets displayed anywhere in the North-East. Bad taste in home decoration seems to go with good taste in food.

I wander down to see the other end of the Stockton to Darlington Railway passing on the way a grocery decorated with a large placard announcing, "We don't cut prices. We murder them!" But nobody is shopping there. They are all at the market. Just by St John's level crossing is the little station where the first railway passenger was booked in 1825 "thus marking an epoch in the history of mankind".

Stockton has two night-clubs, the FIESTA and TITO'S. Tito's is famous all over the North-East and is housed in an Odeon-like monstrosity specially built for it. Personally I prefer Henrico's Bacon Grill which has footprints painted all over the ceiling and where you can order your cup of tea 'big' or 'little'.

As it was Wednesday I wanted to see the cattle market which has now been moved out of the town-centre. I was directed by Sid Staples, chief reporter of the *Darlington & Stockton Times*, now bashing 80, still hard at work, and the proud possessor of an M.B.E. for journalism. No Parish or Rural District Council Meeting in the area ever starts until Sid has arrived and he's an expert on farming.

The 10 or 10a bus from the Town Hall leaves every 15 minutes and you get off at Ashmore, Benson, Pease & Co., the Power-Gas Corporation Ltd. Opposite this is the cattle market and abattoir. "There it is on your left, Pet," says the bus conductor, pointing to his right.

All around the covered auction-ring sheep stand in little pens, eyes popping like cheap yellow beads. They resemble rather silly children waiting trustfully for somebody to explain something. Men in caps lean on the pens saying nowt. The beef-buyers carry long thin sticks and look rich and knowledgeable. The cows have numbers stuck on their rumps and are the only females in sight. I am looked over with interest for signs of foot-and-mouth disease and one or two long thin sticks tremble temptingly within prodding distance of my sirloin.

Inside, the auction-ring is surrounded by concrete tiers on which stand criminally good-looking, tweedy young farmers watching bewildered cattle walking round and round being thwacked on the rump by a ringmaster.

The auctioneer sings a tuneless mumbo-jumbo "Eight-ten

116

eight-fourteen youall gollum vullamum. Two-day diddle hava-
layer eighteen-eighteen-eighteen." A man spits on my foot. In
here I am of no interest to anybody. The man next to the
auctioneer drinks out of a Thermos and takes a sandwich from
tinfoil, looking without pity at poor Buttercup about to breathe
her last in such undignified circumstances. She twitches her ears
and the stick almost hits her in the eye. Poor little white cow, I
mustn't look or I might never be able to eat beef again. At least
nobody tries to hit a lettuce in the eye just before picking it.

Nobody makes the least sign of bidding or of having bought.
There is no evidence of excitement, jealousy, satisfaction. The
auctioneer is young but he looks hard and fierce. Perhaps this is
the psychological result of a lifetime of being horrible to cows.

Buttercup makes way for a little black bull who comes clanking through the weighing machine and runs across to gaze with
pleading great brown orbs right into the face of a cruelly un-
sympathetic farmer on the rails. The little bull gets whacked for
his pains, jumps and turns round in bewilderment. The next
one slips clumsily on to its forelegs then rises to its feet and
strolls over to deposit a large 'pat' right on the shoe of one of
the spectators—after which it departs with simple dignity from
the ring. I enjoyed *that* bit.

A bullock froths at the mouth and moos with fright. "£8. 19.
Anyone a shilling? No?"

"Uh," spits the farmer next to me, tugging at his gold watch-
chain. "Cheap. Cheap."

The atmosphere in an auction-ring is fantastic—something
everybody ought to go and see at least once. But I'd like it better
without the cattle.

Billingham

"You should see Billingham after you've seen the cattle auction," said Sid Staples. "I've been here 53 years now and I remember Billingham when it was just a wicket-gate close to the railway. That was just after I left Wimbledon. Couldn't stand it in Wimbledon. It was too cold and damp. I've only been off work for three days since I moved to Stockton."

So I went to Billingham, now a model town as a result of the rates paid by I.C.I. nearby. There cannot surely be another shopping precinct like the one in Billingham, with pavement underfloor heating. And beat groups, brass bands, and choirs performing there at weekends to keep everybody happy.

There are aviaries in the centre and there is to be a sports forum, new pub, and night club next door. There's a pool, a children's playground, a free 2-level car park. And an Arts Centre for the exhibition of local paintings. When I was there they were showing the El Greco-like pictures by Tom McGuinness, a coal miner. Look out for these while you're up North, and also for the paintings of Norman Cornish. If you're visiting Newcastle you will probably find some in the Stone Gallery (see page 35). These two men are brilliant artists and their pictures are highly evocative—particularly if you, too, have been down a mine.

The I.C.I. building displays in front of it the most lush area of greensward ("Well—we have to. We sell fertiliser, you know!") and inside there are conveyor-belt lifts with no doors, on to which staff and executives leap like ballet-dancers. They don't take itinerant conducted tours round the plant but since there are very few people in south County Durham or the North Riding who don't say "I.C.I." at least once a day either as a subject of praise or blame for anything which might happen to them—from winning the Pools to burning the marmalade—it's as well to know something about it.

The highly-developed Billingham site alone occupies 1,100 acres and this does not count the more recently acquired North Tees and Saltholme Farm site—the first of which now has an oil refinery built on it. Nor, of course, does it include the vast Wilton Works on the South Bank of the Tees, where more than £160 million has been invested since 1945. At Billingham, the Agricultural Division alone produces more than 2½ million tons of chemicals a year, and other I.C.I. divisions on the site account for a further 750,000 tons. All this was born of the First World War when supplies of nitrate needed for the manufacture of explosives were, by 1917, so restricted by the German submarine blockade that Britain's capacity for continuing the war was endangered. The Government then decided to establish a process for manufacturing synthetic nitrogen from the atmosphere on lines similar to the one being used by the enemy. Young scientists who had seen the German methods before the war started worked out the details from memory. The Government chose Billingham as a site because, apart from anything else, it was an area with a surplus of electric power.

Before the process had been fully implemented the U-boat emphasis had switched away, poison-gas was threatened, and the scientists were studying that problem instead. By 1918 the site consisted of a farmhouse, some wooden huts, machinery, the designs for a full-scale factory, and the basic conditions for the production of synthetic ammonia.

By 1920 the site had been bought by Brunner, Mond & Co., and in pursuance of the rest of the country's 'swords into ploughshares' policy the synthetic ammonia process was employed to make fertilisers.

From the seeds of this industry have grown strange plants consisting of enormous pipes, furnaces, retorts, silos, chimneys permanently flaming like Olympic torches, boilers, reformers and pot-bins, all standing somehow rudely undressed in the open air. During the Second World War the 'perspex' invented at Billingham in the mid-30s saved many pilots' lives and the coal

119

I.C.I. made into petrol kept the Hurricanes flying. All the nylon made by I.C.I. in Britain starts at Billingham as 'nylon chips', the research department is about the size of a large factory, and the engineering works employs 3,000 people. Inside the plant are 15 miles of road and approximately 9 miles of railway. Three thousand tons of coal are burned every day and enough electricity is generated to operate the entire London underground. The plant never stops working. Employing three shifts in the local tradition it goes on operating even on Christmas day. Every by-product is used in some way, even the boiler ash finds itself gainfully employed.

They gave me a nice clean paper skull-cap and a tin hat. They explained catalysts, Drikold, urea, and compressions. We climbed ladders which shook under steam-jets. 'Danger, do not touch', it said—as if one would be likely to place one's hand under a jet of boiling steam simply in order to 'touch'. We gazed into the flames of hell screaming white-hot around the pipes. 'This vessel is Hot,' it said. We entered a room throat-searingly sick with ammonia-fumes. 'Half-Hour Breathing-Set', it said. (Rather ominous, this one.) We saw the old white farmhouse right in the middle of the plant, once used as the drawing office, research, and planning department for the old pioneers. Then we went to see something completely beautiful. A big silo storage with a capacity of 100,000 tons where ammonia sulphate fell continually from the high cathedral-like roof in two cascading streams of yellow powder—suddenly utterly silent and utterly purposeful. A huge unbelievable peace in the midst of inferno.

The I.C.I. 'Synthonia Club' is a nice change from the more masculine interests of all excepting the ammonia sulphate silo. It costs 3d a week to join (and a penny for the wife). There's a large, beautifully-decorated lounge leading into a modern bar, darts and games rooms, a Green Room, a billiards room, and a huge theatre-cinema sometimes used as a ballroom. They spend £121,000 on drinks, mostly beer, and the profit from their fruit-machines is £11,000 a year.

Jarrow

Before we take an instructive final drive round County Durham let us visit Jarrow—not to ogle the invisible remains of what everybody once called 'The Hunger March' but to inspect what is not only my own favourite night-club but is also proof positive and proud of the colossal rise to prosperity the North-East has charted over the last six years. The night-club is called CLUB FRANCHI, it cost £60,000 to decorate in 1965 and is the highly lucrative venture of two Franchi and two Volente brothers, all of whom are perfectly charming.

The most amusing manner of reaching it is via the old Tyne Horse Tunnel from North Shields. This is like an underground station, complete with moving staircase of a length similar to that of the sobering heights of Leicester Square, but astonishingly devoid of pretty molls in bras and step-ins. The only notice displayed says "Please Do Not Sit On The Staircase" possibly as a deterrent to inebriates who, having taken one sickening look down, immediately feel inclined to do so.

From here go by way of strange and inimical streets to a nameless pub (which is actually called THE GOLDEN FLEECE) which you can find by getting closer and closer to the sounds made by a piano, a telly, and two jolly barmaids.

A disembodied arm, wearing impeccable gentleman's evening dress, points implacably to the 'LADIES' and the jolly barmaids are called Nellie and Mary. They'll direct you to Jarrow New Town, a modern precinct gay with flowerpots, in the middle of which is the National Assistance Bureau with 'Club Franchi' above it. The club is open every night from

8 p.m. to 2.0 a.m. (10.30 p.m. on Sundays). There is a supper licence until 11.30, a coffee, sandwich, and chicken-leg bar, Newcastle draught beer at about 2d more than in the local, 'Franchi specials' made somewhat pathologically with fresh egg, gin, Italian and white Port (6/-), and 'Rum Snatch'—rum, lime and ginger (5/-). There is also gambling which possibly accounts for its being over the National Assistance Bureau—though I feel it imperative to point out that the two *environs* are not open at exactly the same *moment critique*.

The club is built in a half circle on two floors. It is a prototype of all night-clubs in the North-East, infinitely lush but extremely friendly. All the Dusty Springfields and Gerrys with their Pace-makers, Tommy Coopers and Honeycombes are paid vast sums to entertain in the large cabaret room which is surrounded by 3 coyly-lit bars and has an absolutely marvellous view over the Tyne. During the week sweet little rows of office-party ladies cackle happily and eat enormously at tables around the dance-floor, but on Fridays and Saturdays best clothes and boy-friends are more prominent. Shortly the new Tyne Car Tunnel will open, ending 200 yards from the club, and then possibly best clothes and boy-friends will be an everyday occurrence, but I rather hope not. I liked all these happy little ladies playing Crap in a big red-leather bath, then trotting off with their winnings to buy a drink and a packet of peanuts in Jim's 'Gondolier Bar'.

The night I was there a group called 'The New Faces'—pretty Marie from Dumbarton, and two Charlies (one from Wales and one from Glasgow)—were performing with enormous talent and verve. Fabulous kids they were. The audience loved them. What an opportunity for some vertebrate impresario tired of the sick chicks he has been thrusting to the forefront of the miffling public mind!

One cannot, of course, leave Jarrow without mentioning the church on the site of the monastery founded by Benedict Biscop as a sister establishment to Monkwearmouth. Jarrow is also associated with Bede, who is said to have been taken there by Ceolfrid, first abbot of Jarrow, though the date of Bede's arrival is uncertain. There is a semi-gentle rivalry between Jarrow and Monkwearmouth with regard to Bede and each will firmly deny the other's statements. There is for instance a piece of furniture called 'Bede's Chair' at Jarrow. "Nonsense," say the upholders of Monkwearmouth, "the man who made *that* chair wasn't born when Bede *died*."

In any case, what is certain is that Bede spent his last few years at Jarrow and died there aged 62. He was buried in the South porch of the church until his remains were taken to Durham Cathedral by a certain monk named Elfred. Or they are *said* to have been taken to Durham. Elfred seems to have had a mania for collecting relics and using them as a bait for attracting pilgrims. He visited Jarrow after Bede's death, prayed and fasted alone in the church for several days, and then disappeared early one morning, never to return. Some years later he stated with great assurance that Bede's remains were now in the grave of St Cuthbert and it seems that everybody believed him, much as his extraordinary behaviour—if indeed he did filch the bones from Jarrow—could hardly be termed saintly.

Touring County Durham

Taking the Derwent Valley road from Newcastle through HAMSTERLEY and EBCHESTER, dip down into SHOTLEY BRIDGE which lies mossily below the edge of the Derwent. Unless you're insane about blast furnaces, miss out CONSETT by driving through the afforestation surrounding its outskirts and rejoin the main road at STANHOPE (if you're lost ask for 'Stanopp'). The scenery around here changes from one minute to the next, moors and dales, green fields and farmhouses, sheep crossing, curlews crying. Up to ear-popping heights in undiscovered countryside unchanged for centuries and down to the edge of the river Wear running gently along the edge of the road.

Strike across the moors again to MIDDLETON-IN-TEESDALE and HIGH FORCE, where you might like to have coffee in the High Force Hotel, which has a backyard full of geese and peacocks, before attempting the walk to see the falls.

High Force is a small Niagara belonging to Lord Barnard. For 3d one may enter the wicket gate and walk along the wooded pathway amid the perpendicular basalt rocks, suddenly coming upon this great waterfall, the grandest in England, hurling itself down with enormous strength into the pool below.

Back now to Middleton and through ROMALDKIRK to BARNARD CASTLE. Romaldkirk has a charming little church, 18th-century cottages, green fields and red barns. Next door is COTHERSTONE with narrow streets and daffodils in season on the village green. Round here the occasional house is built of old rust-red brick, a surprise after the more usual yellow-grey stone of most of the buildings further North but not so surprising coming up from the North Riding where red brick takes over almost entirely.

Barnard Castle appears majestically on the other side of a lovely little bridge. William Rufus gave the site of the castle to Guy Baliol in 1098 and the present castle was built by his son, Bernard (hence Barnard) Baliol, in 1112.

But in the 13th century John de Baliol, who founded Balliol College, married the great-niece of William the Lion of Scotland, and that was the end of the family's peaceful occupation of Barnard Castle. When William renounced his fealty to Edward of England in 1293 Barnard Castle was immediately confiscated.

Afterwards this great fortification, whose impressive ruins may be visited via the entrance to the King's Head Hotel where Dickens wrote part of 'Nicholas Nickleby', passed through the hands of many other noble families, Beauchamps, Warwicks, Nevilles. It was associated with royalty when Richard III married Anne Neville.

The town itself is interesting. Scott wrote 'Rokeby' around it and the Elizabethan 'Blagroves House' is worth noting. So is the Town Hall built in 1747.

Just outside is the astonishing building, suddenly rising like Versailles recreated, which houses the BOWES MUSEUM. It is quite indescribably freakish and, although beautiful in itself, somehow in very bad taste. But it should certainly not be missed by any visitor to County Durham.

The history of the museum is very like that of the Wallace Collection in London. It was founded by John Bowes, illegitimate son of the 10th Earl of Strathmore, and his French wife, Countess Josephine Montalbo. The foundation stone was laid in 1869 and the museum opened in 1892. The original idea was to build it in Calais to exhibit the large collection of works of art owned by John and Josephine, but unsettled conditions in France at the time caused them to change their minds if not the design of the building. It is said that it cost £100,000 and I can well understand it.

They picked this site because John had a country seat at Streatlam Castle nearby and (quite obviously) not because they wished large sections of the public to be able to visit their museum, placed as it was almost inaccessibly. Apparently also, Josephine was much younger than her husband and intended to move in and live on the upper floors the minute he died. So, while displaying obedient surface agreement with his ideas and wishes, she still made sure her *oubliette* would be secluded.

Of its more than nine hundred paintings 61 were painted by the Countess herself, a fact obvious even to the most moronic amateur eye. But there are also some excellent Flemish artists represented, and a masterpiece El Greco of 'St Peter'. Devotees of Dr Johnson may be interested in the portrait of Mrs Thrale by Sir Joshua Reynolds. At least, the *head* will have been by Sir Joshua. He had a nasty habit of painting on assembly-line methods and it is thus more than possible that he got somebody else to shove the body in afterwards. There is also a delicious Hogarth of 'Moll Davis'.

The French furniture is lovely, especially the rosewood bureau-dressing-table made for Marie Antoinette's use at Trianon in 1770. So is the pine-panelled gallery taken from Gilling Castle and recreated in the museum.

Having eyed all this, and the ornamental gardens, it may be lunchtime, in which case there's only one place for it. THE GEORGE at PIERCEBRIDGE, another of my favourite hotels in the North-East.

The hotel is extremely comfortable, full of high oak settles, deep fireplaces, and has a delightful country dining-room with bay windows overlooking the river and the bridge. The stables attached to the hotel are partly used for the training of race-horses and the Zetland Hunt meets hereabouts each Tuesday, Thursday and Saturday during the season.

The George Hotel was at one time a staging point for coaches and was in those days kept by two bachelor brothers who had a fine 'long-case' clock, an excellent timekeeper. When one of the brothers died and was buried in the churchyard the clock began to lose and when the other brother died, aged 90, the 'clock stopped, never to go again'.

The story was told to Henry Clay Work, an American composer who visited Piercebridge in the eighties and he wrote the song 'My Grandfather's Clock' which has become the equal of another of his compositions—'Marching Through Georgia'—in international popularity. And the clock that started it all still remains, mute and motionless, in the George Hotel.

I have heard the song sung beautifully by the locals in the pub in Mousehole, Cornwall. But I never heard it sung once in the North-East. Which, considering how fiercely proud they are of their traditional songs and how much they resent classics like 'The Keel Row' being attributed to Glasgow, is odd.

Cut back a little to the West from here to STAINDROP, once the capital of Staindropshire. In 1020 it was given by King Canute to the Patrimony of St Cuthbert after the conclusion of Canute's bare-foot pilgrimage to Durham. After that it had a pretty complicated history, which J. E. Morris tries hard to unravel in his 'Companion into Durham'. With much 'though I cannot make out how' and 'though again by attribution only' or 'we are now in a world of conjecture, or is it purest guess-work?' he winds his way tortuously through Staindrop, Raby Castle close by, and the history of the Nevilles, with special reference to Stain-drop Church. I commend his pages to the really dedicated reader.

BISHOP AUCKLAND is now the only residence of the Bishops of Durham since Van Mildert gave up the castle for a university. It is also, as a good many more people are probably aware, the residence of all the best British Amateur Cup footballers. It is not a pretty place at all—apart from the palace with its grounds —but may possibly interest the reader in having a bit of genuine old Watling Street running South from the market-place.

One has heard so much about the Saxon Church at ESCOMB that one naturally decided now to go and find it. One knows it is near here. But it is not on the map. Finally one finds it—right in the middle of a rather derelict little village, and firmly pad-locked against intruders. Oh, County Durham, proudly regional County Durham! You only let me down once—and this was when. Please do something about your little church at Escomb. There isn't even a sign on it to tell what it is.

Back on the A.1 through SPENNYMOOR, visiting Durham on the way if you have time, taking in PITY ME—a name derived from 'Petit Mer'—the small lake where the monks of Bearpark used to fish for their Friday lunch. To CHESTER-LE-STREET where St Cuthbert's body lay for 100 years until another Danish raid in 995 sent it again on the journey which ended in Durham.

And so, for the purpose of this particular book, back across the Tyne to Newcastle.

Part Three

---※---

THE NORTH RIDING
OF YORKSHIRE

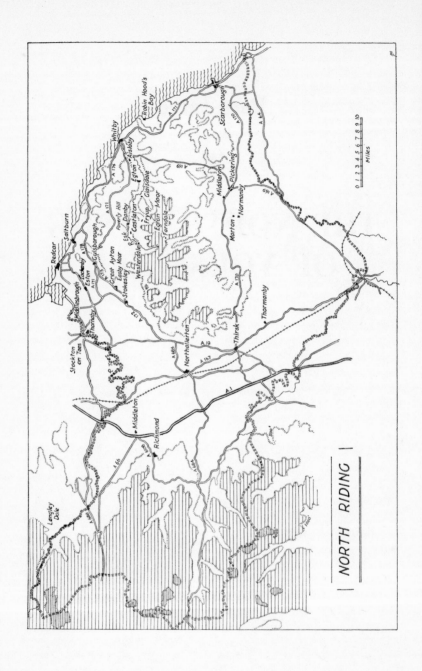

NORTH RIDING

A Short History

Ask any Londoner and he'll know Yorkshire is in England. Ask him how he knows and he'll probably say, "Cricket and pudding." Ask him what the Yorkshire Ridings are and he'll say, "The Brontës." His replies may depress one—but at least he does know where Yorkshire is.

Yorkshire is the largest shire in England, half as large as Belgium. And it is divided into three 'Ridings'. The North Riding is the fourth largest county in England with an area of 1,361,788 acres and only the West Riding, Lincolnshire, and Devonshire are (in that order) larger.

For our purposes the North Riding is part of the North-East coast. But it provides less of astonishment than the rest to the Southerner since it consists more of the green fields and red-brick houses he is used to, though he may find the dialect even more difficult to understand than he did the 'Geordie'. It is much harder, broader, flatter.

The other thing the Londoner will know about Yorkshire is that it has 'Dales'. In fact the Dales form part of the Yorkshire National Park, which is in the North Riding. There is nothing in England like a true Yorkshire Dale, consisting as it does of long, broad valleys strewn with villages almost cut off from the rest of the world but excellently in communication with one another.

The Celts twice invaded the North Riding, the second invasion consisting of the Welsh-sounding Cymri who left traces of occupation in the moorlands. At the time of the Roman invasion the paradoxically French-sounding Brigantes were exclusively, and extremely warlikely, peopling the area and their ferocity may be judged from the Roman tag, 'Dirue Maurorum attegias, castella Brigantum'.

York is not in the North Riding area but it was almost an 'altera Roma' since it was where Hadrian resided, Severus was cremated, and Constantine the Great was proclaimed.

The invaders arrived and Ida proclamed his throne at Bamburgh. Yorkshire, under the name of Deira, was the Southern extremity of this kingdom which extended from the Humber to the Forth. Christianity—such as it had been—retired with the conquered natives and was only revived with the arrival of Ethelburga and Paulinus to Northumberland in 617. Thereafter the Christian era in Yorkshire coincided with that in Northumberland and County Durham.

The North Riding was dotted with monasteries, the most famous being at Whitby, but these shrines were doomed to violent destruction with the arrival of the Danes, and one of the last Scandinavian invasions of Yorkshire was in 1066 when Harold Hadrada fell at Stamford Bridge. A few days later Harold of England met his own end at Battle and the Norman conquest began.

Earl Godwin was lord of the 5 great wapentakes ('weapontakes') which constituted the area and were called Richmondshire. The present 'Riding' is a corruption of 'Trithing'—a third part or division—which occurred then or a little earlier, with the end of the Danish occupation.

In 1069 came the reckless massacre of the Norman garrison at York, startling William the Conqueror out of his composure, and all the inhabitants of the North-East from York upwards out of their wits. Everywhere the country was laid waste. In a Domesday survey made 15 years later entry after entry stated, "vastum est".

Now commenced the great castle-building era which continued through three succeeding reigns. Many of these fortresses were subsequently taken from the turbulent barons by Henry II. But side by side with them had grown beautiful abbeys and humble monastic cells. Altogether, fourteen of these had been founded in the North Riding alone before the close of the Norman occupation.

Then came the Scottish incursions, inspiring terror and laying the lands to waste once more. Three of these battles were fought in the North Riding—in 1138, 1319, and 1322. The Wars of the Roses started in 1455 and was followed by abortive rebellions culminating in the dissolution of the smaller monasteries by Henry VIII in 1536 and the rest in 1539. At the same time came 'The Pilgrimage of Grace' and the great 'Rising of the North' rooted in religious grievances. The Civil War found the king in York since Yorkshire was for the most part royalist, and the battle of Marston Moor was fought there. Yorkshire also possessed the last two strongholds to battle on for the king—Scarborough and Pontefract.

We shall earn salty observations from the North Riding if we fail to mention the iron in the Cleveland Hills, much as my type of reader is more likely to be interested in the fact that the Yorkshire Dales National Park is a good place for starting the Pennine Walk if one doesn't want to do the whole 250 miles. An excellent map of the walk, just the right size for a sporty rucksack, may be obtained free from the National Parks Commission, 1, Cambridge Terrace, N.W.1 (WEL 0366).

Middlesbrough

Though the small, attractive, agricultural town of NORTH-ALLERTON is the County Town and administrative centre of the North Riding, it is MIDDLESBROUGH—as the capital of the rapidly developing 'County Borough of Teesside'—which is of more astounding interest to the newcomer.

Say 'Teesside' to the Londoner and he looks completely blank. Explain to him that the largest industrial area in Great Britain is in the process of forming itself, and that, by 1967, Middlesbrough, Billingham, Eston, Stockton, Thornaby, and Redcar will in fact be collectively known as 'Teesside' and he will gibber with fright. He may not have the remotest conception of what *Newcastle* is really like, but he certainly understands Middlesbrough, Billingham, Eston, Stockton, Thornaby, and Redcar. And collectively he finds them faintly menacing.

Which is why we are starting with Middlesbrough.

The Yorkshireman is completely different from any other man anywhere else in the North-East, and Middlesbrough is exactly as the Londoner imagines it. If I say, "where there's moock there's brass," however, I would not wish my readers to imagine that there's any moock in Middlesbrough. In fact Middlesbrough is almost kinky in its provision of blue-and-yellow, spotlessly clean litter bins at every conceivable and inconceivable spot. But there's certainly 'brass' there and the Yorkshireman is, rightly, fiercely proud of the fact. If he knocks down some of his historical landmarks to make way for yet another factory who's to say he isn't absolutely correct in the long run? And like any other town in the North-East, the outskirts of Middlesbrough are very pretty, there are plenty of inexpensive brand-new houses with front and back gardens 10 minutes from the town centre, and the sea is just around the corner.

The Middlesbroughian has by far the best fish-and-chips, the crustiest new master-baked bread, and his women have the amplest bosoms. His sausages, flicked with a twist of the wrist into appropriate lengths before your very eyes, are the tastiest, his Newbould's pies the freshest, meatiest, best-filled, and crunchiest. All his cakes are 'gateaux' thickly piled with fruit, fresh cream, jelly and angelica. His draught beer is the strongest in the country, brewed specially to be served on the job to the steelworkers who perspire so much. His night-life rollicks from Monday to Sunday at the CONTESSA (among others). And his town sports as many Building Societies as it does pubs.

His buses are blue-painted and are lettered instead of numbered. The older ones have seats on a platform to one side of the top deck which makes it terribly difficult for the conductresses to collect their fares and terribly easy for the passengers to knock themselves silly against the roof when rising to get off.

Middlesbrough itself is efficiently tearing itself down and shoving itself up again. Its streets are straight, flat, and uncompromising, but they are also almost totally jam-less. Nobody could call the town beautiful—but criticise it at your peril! The kindness of the Middlesbroughian is rough and broad, like his vowels, and he gives immense sums to charity. But he doesn't like any suggestion that the pale green and yellow clock in ALBERT PARK would be much improved by an ambulatory musical toucan like the Guinness clock in Battersea Pleasure Gardens. And he looks like a pathetically disappointed little boy if he sends you off to admire an iron foundry (oddly rusty) at Thornaby and you go wandering elsewhere by mistake, returning at teatime to say you thought Yarm was simply splendid.

When one considers that Middlesbrough was only invented in 1830 and that, in 1829, the total population numbered only 40, one cannot but admire the speed at which it has grown. One can also begin to understand the Londoner's unease.

Taking not the slightest notice of any directions, which nearly always include "oop be th'Gaumont" because they've forgotten they took the Gaumont to pieces last week, make your way to the ART GALLERY in Linthorpe Road if only to admire the riveting notice therein which states, 'No Smoking. No Dogs. No Ice-Creams.' and to the rather charming little DORMAN MEMORIAL MUSEUM. This was built by Sir Arthur Dorman in memory of his son and the men of the Princess of Wales's Own Yorkshire Regiment who fell with him in the South African War. The natural history section is particularly interesting, especially the 10-foot stuffed Ribbon Fish taken in 1866 at Seaton Carew, enough to put one off paddling *there* again for a month or two. The marine section is pleasing and the parquet smells deliciously of muskily expensive floor-polish and the dear dead housemaids of my youth, rubbing away so long before breakfast.

Opposite the museum is REA'S CREAMY ICES PARK BAR which looks pretty gloomy from the outside but has a grotto complete with real waterfall inside. It also has Rea's Creamy Ices, which most certainly are and may even be one extremely good reason for the notice in the Art Gallery.

I must also recommend the GINGHAM KITCHEN oop be th'Gaumont where the prices are in inverse ratio to the really delightful décor and the excellent meals quickly served on individual trays bearing little serviettes inscribed, "Good Morning, Madam!" I don't know if they have a 'Sir' as well because I didn't have one with me at the time. But I'm almost certain they will have.

As to the history of the town, I had to get that from Mr Lillie, the ex-Chief Librarian, thus: "Middlesbrough has had an almost continuous history since 1119 when the Robert de Brus of Skelton Castle left land and money for the good of the souls of himself and his wife to the Cell of Middleburg on condition that some Benedictine Monks resided in the Cell for all time, which, until the Dissolution, they did. At least three of these monks became abbots at Whitby.

"In 1133 there was a dispute between Whitby and Guisborough as to who should receive the tithes from Middleburg Cell. De Brus called them together and they decided Middleburg should be the mother church and that the tithes should go to Whitby. In 1366 there was another dispute because some of the monks of Middleburg revolted against the Abbey of Whitby for taking too much from Middleburg and impoverishing the priory church. In his turn the Abbot accused the monks of Middleburg of leaving the Cell without permission and disclosing the secrets of the Order to the ordinary people. One, Peter de Hertilpool, was accused in particular. But this was settled in 1393 when Peter became abbot of Whitby.

"In 1537 the abbot of Whitby attended a convocation at York and when he returned he was asked what news he had. His news was ominous. Anne Boleyn was trying to force Henry VIII to take the jewels and chalices away from the churches. He resigned as abbot because of these signs, took his pension, and returned to the Cell at Middleburg where he had once been an anchorite. He turned the Cell into a farm in 1660 and was thus the first tenant of Middleburg Farm which the Pease family bought in 1828 to turn into a coal-exporting port."

Mr Lillie spent considerable years as a Librarian looking up all this information, and a great deal more of what happened before, as he put it, "iron crept out of the Cleveland Hills, where it had slept since Roman days, like an invincible serpent. And it coiled itself round the world."

He told me that, in 1871, the 40,000 population of Middlesbrough included 1,669 people from the West Midlands, 1,531 from Wales, 1,365 from Scotland, and 3,622 from Ireland.

"No wonder," he sadly added, "they'll keep their Oldest Furnace and demolish their oldest building."

Alas, yes. But who is to say that this might not also be the only means of keeping one's head above the onrush of an unfamiliar modern tide?

Sports in the area are manifold and the Middlesbrough Little Theatre, opened in 1957, provides the panacea of culture. Further education and recreation is covered by 'Signpost'—a booklet produced by the Middlesbrough Education Committee, which covers anything from the 'British Association for the Advancement of Science' to the gentler arts indulged in by the 'Teesmouth Bird Club'. To which I might add that the birds round Teesside include kestrel hovering, tern skimming, and the absolutely fantastic sight of 10,000 knots suddenly rising and turning as one—like a swarm of locusts but infinitely more beautiful and less destructive.

If you like to stay in a friendly place, try STUDLEY HOUSE, 13, The Crescent, 5 minutes by bus from the town centre. It's a jolly 'theatrical digs' where you may find Dusty Springfield or

Max Wall sitting in the kitchen with a cup of tea. It is run on highly informal lines by Laurie and Margaret Jacobs. Unfortunately they've stopped serving meals though you may be able to wheedle one of the best plates of home-made thick *potage* you've ever had in Britain from Margaret if you're good at wheedling and she's not too fraught. The sides of bacon hanging from the ceiling prompted me to ask Laurie—who was once a butcher—about real York Ham. Somebody had told me the pigs were fed on the ullage from the local beer to make them sleepy and fat and too drunk to bother to eat their young. This seemed cruel and unreasonable. Except for their young, of course.

"York ham called York Ham frequently isn't York Ham at all," said Laurie. "Good York Ham is made from sows who have had a litter. They are killed and dry cured—the rest are wet cured. Then they are put on a slab, their veins are plugged with saltpetre, and they are rubbed all over with salt. And the result is hanging up there."

Well, this seems pretty cruel and unreasonable too, really. Because this way they aren't even allowed to get *drunk* before swinging from the ceiling.

Two good places for meals while staying at Studley House are the LINTHORPE HOTEL opposite, where pretty Marjorie makes melba toast properly rolled as you never seem to get it in London and worries about being over-tipped. And the POVERINA HOTEL in NORMANBY, where you must book (Normanby 272) for a proper family-type Sunday lunch which you can't get at the Linthorpe.

Margaret Jacobs drove me to a real Working Men's Club a little out of town because I wanted to see one in action.

The room was like a huge dormitory at an inexpensive boarding-school. There were hardly any women there and the men looked awfully serious. They wore flat 'ats, all right—but of the modern sporty type with the crown stitched to the visor.

A member of the club appeared on stage. "Now Ladies and GentleMEN. I am about to introduce for your enter-TAIN-ment . . . uh . . . ,' he starts fishing through his pockets . . . "*straight* from radio and tele-VIS-ion . . . uh . . ." he produces a scruffy piece of paper, looks extremely relieved, and announces the artiste.

There is no applause. Everybody looks dour. They're not going to look pleased until they see what they're getting for their brass. This would completely unseat the reason of any non-professional, which is why only the top artistes ever appear at Working Men's Clubs.

Nor is there any laughter until the comedian has finished his act. He comes on after the singer and his patter is very blue indeed. The moment he has finished the excitement is over-powering. He is clapped on the back, congratulated. "Eeee Maxie. I loooved thaaat!" All is well. It was worth the brass after all. Break for musicians. Pints of Newcastle Brown Ale all round. Everybody looks terribly relieved. The comedian looks positively maudlin.

For the second half of the show there is more enthusiasm due to Newcastle Brown Ale and satisfied appreciation at the proper employment of brass. The comedian's wife comes on in a bathing costume and performs some fractionally improper acrobatics. Everybody settles back, clapping madly and emitting 'Eeee's' of pure enjoyment.

Nobody took the slightest notice of Margaret and me. Possibly we should have worn bathing suits.

But the thing everybody must do in Middlesbrough is to cross the Tees on the meccano-type Transporter, an experience you will get nowhere else in the world.

The bus takes you to the bridge and you pay 1d at a toll-gate. You then board the bridge on the little railway-carriage-type covered platform. "Doan't hurry, Pet," drawls the conductor. "I never like to be hurried meself!"

Feeling much as they must do when crossing from East to West Germany you wonder if you should have brought your passport, while anxiously counting the heavy vehicles piling in on the ramp in the middle. Everybody looks uncommonly cheerful and relaxed. Perhaps they haven't noticed the thin wire from which you appear to be suspended?

Off goes the bridge, clanking ponderously across the pale-grey slime and affording an uninterrupted view of large expanses of the general moock the brass comes from.

Once safely delivered in County Durham perhaps you'd like to take my favourite bus-ride? It's the one between the Transporter and Seaton Carew. I did it 6 times, if only for the appalling thrill of never being entirely certain I'd ever get there. Or back.

The road is said to have been made by the 1914 German prisoners-of-war who fixed the camber in such a way as to ensure final retribution. The bus arrives and squats before the Transporter, panting. You board it and sit on top, innocently unaware that you should not only have brought your seat-belt but almost certainly fastened it. Suddenly the bus makes up its mind, and with a deep sigh and a sickening lurch decides to make one last hopeless attempt to reach civilisation.

You do not progress in the normal fashion symbolised by the word . . . you attempt a series of bus-borne pole-vaults between mud-flats which can only have been invented by Tennessee Williams in the course of one of his most sombre excogitations. Derelict cars, broken fences, lonely petrol-stations appear and disappear like the phantasmagoria of a deranged mind. Suddenly the bus grinds to a horrible halt by a poor, depressed little pipe which is pouring water into a hole by the side of the road, totally unaware that it had already managed to fill the hole up with water years and years ago. This hole is now pouring the same water back into another hole—behind and out of sight of the poor, depressed little pipe which is continuing to pour water out of the second hole into the first hole in a pathetically ghastly attempt to be of *some* use to *somebody*.

Nobody ever gets on or off the bus here, mainly because the idea of being left in such a nightmare spot would be even more terrifying than attempting to continue the journey to Seaton Carew. So the bus obviously only stops here due to some odious moral it wishes to point at its passengers.

Thereafter it vagabonds madly past orderly rows of little huts standing in a waterlogged field, each hut with its own tiny telegraph pole, possibly for the transmitting of messages to St Bernard dogs in midwinter. As it nears its destination the bus bucks like a Arab steed smelling Turkish Delight, and suddenly realising that it has *indeed* managed the journey yet once more, jerks to a sulky stop, looks hopefully round for its lump of sugar, and squats inimically down again waiting for just *one* more person to *dare* it to return. *Ever.*

Guisborough

Just outside Middlesbrough are the lovely ruins, excellently well-preserved, of the Augustinian Priory founded here in 1119 by Robert de Brus 'counselled and admonished' by Pope Calixtus. De Brus was the first lord of Skelton and of a large part of North Cleveland, and Guisborough was one of the wealthiest religious houses in England at the time of the Dissolution when it was valued at £628 3s 4d.

In 1289 it was burned down 'due to the carelessness of a plumber at work on the roof', though it is difficult to discover what exactly the plumber did. He can't have been lighting a fag so possibly he was just trying to keep warm.

Twenty years at least elapsed before the priory was rebuilt and its erstwhile magnificence may be judged by the really glorious East end through the portals of which one discovers a wonderful framed view of the surrounding countryside.

In Murray's 'Handbook for Yorkshire' written in 1904 is a description of how the priory must once have looked, which ends in a fascinating piece of information. "The kitchen is at the S.W. corner of the frater and in the W. cloister is a good Dec. lavatory," declares Mr Murray.

By turning back to the 'Principal Abbreviations' one discovers that 'Dec.' stands for 'Decorated Gothic Style (1270 to 1370: Edward II and Edward III).'

The ruins are situated in beautiful gardens in which a chestnut tree, said to be over 600 years old, droops its branches to the ground. Wherever they have touched they have rooted and sprung up as independent trees. From the garden may be seen

Roseberry Topping, which sounds like the latest plastic ice-cream improver but is in fact a conical hill about which there is an old weather-saying which goes, "When Roseberry Topping wears a cap, Cleveland may beware a clap."

Those wishing to work in Middlesbrough and live in the country might do worse than to look around the outskirts of Guisborough, once a mere hamlet for the accommodation of Cleveland iron-diggers but now a small country town in pretty surroundings, well-endowed with brand-new houses—each one different.

Redcar

This is the perfect seaside town, 30 minutes from Middlesbrough with all the amenities of a small one and none of the vulgarities of a large one. From here Brighton seems stuffy and horribly overcrowded.

You may take it as you will. As a holiday resort, in which case there are miles of sandy golden beaches, good shops, roller-skating if you must, and wildly expensive Knickerbocker Glories entirely concocted at the whim of the waitress. The PARK HOTEL on the front, run by Reg and Betty Wilson, is excellent. Rooms with telephone are around £2 bed-and-breakfast and the bars are decorated with photographs of familiar faces signed, "Love from Pearl and Teddy" or "Thanks for a lovely weekend."

Or you may decide to live there, in which case you cannot possibly help meeting the incredibly beautiful 6-foot Thompson brothers, Jim and Mark, who live in 'Fisherman's Square' ("inshore fishing, Pet") and stride about the place refusing to get married, thereby driving the girls—both holiday and local—to the edge of neurasthenia.

Jim has a shock of curly grey hair and wears one of those pale-blue denim windcheaters most clench-bottomed Chelsea lassies will sit for hours in the bath in, trying to fade them to the fashionable colour. Mark is blond and wears the same type of garment in rust red.

"We're getting a 33-foot Yorkshire coble built, Pet, with a Kelvin-Hughes Echo-Meter for detecting lobsters. It's unfair on the lobsters but every boat is mechanised now and you can't miss."

"Will the lobsters be cheaper, then?"

"No. They're getting very scarce on account of all this mechanisation, Pet. But it cuts the labour. You can't get the young men to come out in the morning to bait long lines with 12 to 15 score hooks and 2 to 3 mussels to a hook. We have to open the mussels first too, you see. So we stick to lobster-fishing, then you don't need help ashore, see? Look at me fists though! I didn't get them cracking lobsters, no Pet, you're right! Picking up a pint's what did it."

The Thompsons' grandfather was coxswain of the 'Zetland' lifeboat which is still preserved in Redcar. "He won the Champion Cup and 100 guineas in 1873 rowing 4-handed from Redcar buoy to Saltdean Pier, 7 miles in 14½ minutes. Somebody tried to buy the trophy off us . . ." Jim spits. "*Uh!*"

I ask him about North-Eastern superstitions. "No, we don't mind taking women to sea but we think it's bad luck to see them on our way out in the morning. But we start round 5.0 a.m. so we don't often see any."

"Oh no, no, *no*, Pet. We never fish on Sunday. It's bad luck. Nine out of 10 fishermen can't swim, see? I can't swim and I went over the wall on a Sunday once. I dropped seven fathoms and I thought I'd never get shot o' me drop o' water."

The information that 9 out of 10 fisherman can't swim completely stuns me. "How almost idiotically courageous," I say.

Jim roars with happy laughter. "Uh," he says, "she's *nice!*" To cheer me up he tells me a story about having "twelve bottles in me seaboots" and the Customs man saying "it was the cleverest bloody move he'd ever seen in his life." Somebody else tells me about Tom Smith from Redcar who formed a mouth-organ band of the unemployed when 'times were bad' and taught them to play music, after which they represented Great Britain in 'the world championships of 1938'.

I am escorted to the QUEEN'S HOTEL at Saltburn which appears to be the only place in the entire North-East where they sell White Shield Worthington—my favourite drink—and Jim insists that I drink Carlsberg Lager. "Makes holes in your seaboot stockings," he firmly states. He informs me that the stone used to build Covent Garden was shipped from Whitby and tells me about going to give evidence in an arbitration case at the Law Courts. "There were more lies told in that courtroom

. . . my solicitor kept pulling me down . . . well, Pet, vou're not allowed to *speak*. I wasn't going to allow them to get away with *that*." Before I discover whether he won his case or not he suddenly states, "There's more fish caught in the Royal public house in Redcar than anywhere else. They're in it up to their chests. You should have met Tosher. He could strike matches on his wrists." Suddenly he glares at the barmaid. "Get your finger out of the measure, lass!" he booms. "You couldn't catch two men's breakfasts."

"I saved 23 people once and 36 at another in me own boat. I've got nothing against the lifeboats, not after me Dad was in it so long. But the fishermen have to help too, see?"

"But you don't get anything for it," I said.

"Get anything? GET anything?" cried Jim. "I don't want *paying*. These rocks round here are dangerous. In the days of wooden boats 28 were wrecked in 16 hours once. Once after a rescue a woman come and give me a roll of notes. 'That's yours,' she says. 'Get off the sands,' I says, 'and take your money with you.'" Suddenly he gave his huge laugh another run. "She come back," he said, "and give me a dozen sticks of Redcar Rock instead!"

If you go to Redcar you might find Jim and Mark Thompson now in 'Sea Lover II' which they hoped to launch last August.

Mr Laurie Picknett of Picknett's Fish Shop in the High Street told me the story of the 'Zetland'.

"Britain was the first place in the world to do something about lifeboats," he said. "Until then people just stood helplessly by, watching people drown. In 1789 the 'Adventure' ran ashore at South Shields in heavy seas no boat could survive. The gentlemen in the club room at the Law House overlooking the sea just stood watching bodies being swept away. They originated a competition for plans for 'unsubmersible' boats which would survive heavy broken shoal water and save lives.

"A South Shields housepainter and Sunday School teacher, Willy Wouldhave, Henry Greathead, a carpenter, and several more people put in good ideas. Willy Wouldhave was only offered half the winning money and stalked out! So Greathead was offered the job of incorporating all the ideas into something to be called a 'lifeboat'. He built the 'Original' which was an instant success. He won awards and acclaim and in 1816, when he died, he had built 30 lifeboats altogether. In 1830, in a terrible storm, the 'Original' was wrecked after saving hundreds of lives. And all the rest went too with the exception of the 'Zetland'."

These lifeboats were horse-drawn to the beach and rowed by ten unpaid local fishermen. Nowadays maroons crack over the town but in those days they were called by an Alarm Drum, one of which is in the museum. In the heaviest weather they might be 'double-bunked' and 20 men would row. If they were drowned nothing official was done for their dependents.

But motorisation took over and the 'Zetland' was condemned to be broken up. The fishermen who loved her intervened and after 80 years service she was bought by the people of Redcar and housed in the museum given to them by Emma Dawson with its clubroom and lookout tower on top.

"The old coxswain, Johnny Stonehouse, retired in 1965 after 63 years of unbroken service. His great-grandfather was in the 'Zetland'," said Laurie Picknett. "But his son's gone into the air force."

As I stood looking at the brave little 'Zetland' in its museum in Redcar I wondered if one could really blame Johnny's son. The Royal National Lifeboat Institution returned to voluntary service after 15 years in the last century when it received a Government grant. The Government imposed a number of conditions, as governments have to when they grant money, but the system didn't work, as sometimes it doesn't. The lifeboats are now back as a service given almost for nothing by courageous men in their own time. There are 150 lifeboats around the 5,000 mile long coasts of Britain and Ireland. They have rescued about 85,000 people since 1824, an average of 50 a month, or 11 every week. The service costs over 1½ million pounds a year (or £150 every hour). At each lifeboat station there is one full-time member of the crew—the motor mechanic. The other members, normally 8 men, earn their living in other ways. The coxswain, second coxswain, and bowman receive small retaining fees and the coxswain is in complete command while the boat is at sea. Lifeboats today are more than twice as busy as they were 30 years ago. In 1964 they put to sea 929 times.

I think I will not speak of how much money they 'earn' and how much pension they 'get'. They have a certain dignity which is deserving of respect. They never think of going on strike and the glory or reward of their dangerous calling can only be described as sickening. Next time you see them around London in their oilskins, collecting rather shyly for themselves, just remember one thing. I will.

Supposing one day we need them? Won't we feel awfully guilty if we didn't even bother to give them 6d? There have been some pretty nasty inshore accidents lately.

How It's Done

Around the North Riding it is even more essential to admire men at work than it is in Newcastle. Mainly because almost every man in Middlesbrough weighs in at the drop of a diphthong with, "Have you see any of our industry yet?"

This book being mainly for women, who are apt to back away hissing with fright when the word 'industry' is mentioned, I suggest two of the more interesting visits which might be undertaken, thus ensuring that the next time she is asked the inescapable question the poor girl can reply "Yes" and have done with it.

A visit to DORMAN LONG at LACKENBY is not easy to achieve but it is more than possible that by 'industry' most Yorkshiremen mean 'steel' in some form or another.

It is said that 'iron-puddling' was started by the monks at Rievaulx Abbey. In that case they certainly started *something*. Dorman Long now employ 25,000 people, about 18,000 of them on Teesside in iron and steel production.

Unfortunately, due to shortage of time on the part of both Dorman's and myself, I had to pay a very hurried visit. I shot past pig-iron, crude steel, blast furnaces, 'bleeders', railway lines, 'down-comers' full of gas, Bessemer furnaces, naked flames, rusty coke-ovens, miles of ingot moulds, electric arc furnaces, huge sorcerers' ladles full of sparks, steel joists, girders, the whole thing overhung by the tangy, exciting smell of iron.

We entered a building in which red-hot rivers of molten steel were being poured into ingot moulds of a size big enough to make jellies for Gargantua. Enormous ladles tipped the bright crimson liquid and huge tongs picked up the steel joists and girders.

It is obvious that in order to keep this colossal plant going, Dorman Long no sooner finish one job than they must start another immediately. I have read all the arguments for and against the Steel Bill. None has so far convinced me that *any* government can run Dorman Long better than Dorman Long can. If we're not very careful it seems to me we'll be back at iron-puddling.

The other fascinating visit is the one you make to your own underclothing at FOISTER, CLAY & WARD, who make smalls for Marks & Spencer on the outskirts of the brand-new airport at MIDDLETON.

Summer thin and winter thick, elephants' vests are knitted into long tubes to be cut up later into the pretty little snugs you buy in Oxford Street. Bobbins go round and round like a mad fairground in a room attended by approximately two people—one of whom is probably the cleaner. Red pantalettes you'll be wearing next season are chopped with lethal blades through 24 thicknesses. Four-needled little sewing machines buzz like bees adding the pretties to your panties. Shirts, sweaters, thick-knits and T-shirts are fully-fashioned by girls earning £20 a week on piece-work. Marks & Spencer command 50 per cent of the sweater-market, so I'm told, and this has never surprised me. For a start I wouldn't dare to drop dead in the street in any undies other than those bearing a St Michael's label and secondly I can't wait for Foister, Clay & Ward's sugar-pink fully-fashioned thick-knits to appear down South.

Richmond

Without any doubt Richmond is the most romantic place in the whole of the North-East. The Swale in a rocky bed flows round the hill upon which stands the great stronghold of Alan the Red, one of the sons of the Duke of Brittany, who came over with William the Conqueror. These lands were given to the Breton earl after Eadwine's last revolt in 1072 which ended in his death.

Earl Alan called his castle 'Richemunde' meaning 'strong hill' and Richmond became the capital of Richmondshire, which consisted of 164 manors in Yorkshire. But the first Earl of Richmond had in his 'honour' 440 manors altogether scattered throughout England.

The fourth Earl of Richmond married the heiress of the Breton dukedom and thus became both Earl and Duke. It was his son, Conan, who built the massive Keep now cresting the precipice above the river and who married Margaret, sister of Malcolm IV of Scotland. His daughter was the Lady Constance in Shakespeare's 'King John', the mother of Arthur and Eleanor.

The Dukes of Brittany retained their English lands only off and on since each time England and France went to war the Bretons attached themselves to France and had their properties confiscated. They were taken away for the last time in the reign of Richard II and the castle passed to the Earl of Westmorland. The earldom, however, was given to Edmund Tudor eldest son of Owen Tudor and Queen Katharine. His son, Henry VII, claimed the title of Earl of Richmond through John of Gaunt, to whom it had been given by Edward III, and transferred the name to the palace of Sheen he had rebuilt on the banks of the Thames. In fact it appears that the 'Lass of Richmond Hill' who is commemorated by a large public house next to the park in Surrey was in fact a Yorkshire lass named Frances l'Anson who had never even heard of Ham Common.

From the castle stretches one of the most magnificent views in the North-East, over the foaming river, up Swaledale, to the distant towers of York. Under the rock King Arthur and his knights are said to lie 'spellbound in mysterious sleep'. A certain Potter Thompson once penetrated their hideout where he found them unconscious before a great table on which rested a horn and a sword. He began to draw the sword when, to his terror, a voice suddenly boomed:

> "Potter, Potter Thompson
> If thou hadst either drawn
> The sword, or blown the horn
> Thou'd been the luckiest man
> That ever yet was born."

Poor Potter Thompson. One does sympathise with him in his subsequent demented rush for the exit. But he must often in later life have wished he'd stayed once he'd sat down quietly and worked out what that voice actually *had* said.

The town itself is lovely, preserving a mediaeval aspect to a quite unexpected degree. One is conscious of the neighbourhood of miles of lonely moorland. The chapel of Holy Trinity in the wide cobbled market-place is set about with houses and shops. The tower of Grey Friars also merits inspection; the graceful remains of a Franciscan church, founded in 1258 by Ralph Fitz-Ranulph, which was surrendered after determined opposition by a prior and fourteen brethren to the demands of Henry VIII.

One of the most charming buildings is that of the Georgian Theatre in Frenchgate. It was built and opened by the actor-manager Samuel Butler in 1788 with a production which started by his reading a prologue, followed by a comedy and a comic opera which had been performed in London only a few months before. It was used by strolling players and between 1830 and 1848 both Edmund and Charles Kean and Ellen Tree appeared there. Performances became less frequent and finally it was let as an auction room, corn chandler's store, and furniture repository. In the Second World War it became a salvage depot. The auditorium was floored over flush with the stage and the pit turned into wine vaults.

In 1960 the Georgian Theatre (Richmond) Trust Ltd. was formed and restoration began. The enthusiasm of local residents who gave, and still give, their services free helped restore it to its former shape, a tiny gem, a masterpiece of atmosphere. The Society of Theatrical Craftsmen and Designers lent in perpetuity the oldest scenery extant in England, painted in 1836. No other playhouse can give the authentic atmosphere of a period piece written for a stage whereon actors and audience are in the closest company in the enchantment of a performance with a re-creation of the original candlelight. The tiny boxes, red, gold-studded, are named Dryden, Congreve, Sheridan. The box-office is still the original small recess and counter.

It is open only during the summer from the month of May, and two voluntary helpers are there to show visitors round from 2.30 p.m. to 5.0. The 2/6d booklet written by Richard Southern and Ivor Brown is extremely interesting, particularly for Ivor Brown's lively description of acting and actors from the strolling players onwards.

Touring The North Riding

The North Riding of Yorkshire does not have Alice in Wonderland but—again to the surprise of the Londoner (who thinks he has everything)—it does have Captain Cook.

Drive from Middlesbrough to STOKESLEY, straight into the Cleveland Hills and you will see the Cook Monument atop EASBY MOOR. It is a tall column somewhat resembling Cleopatra's Needle and you can draw a bead on it by looking first for Roseberry Topping (see page 142). Thereafter you must make a slight detour to reach GREAT AYTON, a pretty little place strung round two large village greens. Cook was born in the neighbouring village of MARTON but was educated at Great Ayton (once known as 'Canny Yatton') and his schoolroom is preserved inside the building of the Yorkshire Bank. There is no plaque over the building itself and one has to go round the corner of the bank to discover over the little door, 'Michael Osgood Built this School House in the Year 1704. Rebuilt 1785.' Cook lived between 1728 and 1779.

Near the banks of the river Leven, which runs somewhat thinly through the village, is the CAPTAIN COOK CAFÉ. It would be a pity to allow this to put you right off it since this is where you will get the very, *very* best fish-and-chips you have ever eaten in all your life, cooked in spotlessly clean surroundings and properly wrapped in greaseproof and newspaper to be eaten *al fresco*. A little wooden fork is provided for their more fastidious customers.

Morris in his 'North Riding of Yorkshire' (written in 1906) describes "the new church" in Great Ayton as having "nave arcades all as bad as bad can be, and a roof of slated hideousness." But what I love most about Mr Morris's description is that he adds that Grace Cook 'mother of the circumnavigator' is buried in the churchyard with several of his brothers and sisters. I wonder what Captain Cook would have thought about being described as a 'circumnavigator' in its more modern usage.

You are now in the NORTH YORK MOORS NATIONAL PARK, about 353,920 acres of open moorland. You may not wish to follow me. If it is the month of April possibly you'd prefer to drive over to see the 5 miles of daffodils positively bouncing out of the ground all over FARNDALE. In this case, write to the TEESSIDE INDUSTRIAL DEVELOPMENT BOARD, 1A, Darlington Street, Thornaby-on-Tees, for lists of hotels and prices and for any other information they may think relevant to your journey.

My drive takes you over purple moor thick with pheasant and grouse. You will pass hunts and point-to-points, smell the heady perfume of green fields, fir, and yellow gorse. You will switchback up hills and into valleys peopled exclusively by very fat hens and the Black-Face and Swaledale sheep used for the manufacture of Harris Tweed, taking in on the way marvellous panoramic views just before reaching CASTLETON on the salmon-rich Esk. This is Upper and Lower WESTERDALE, full of small villages spilling down the hillsides, the quintessence of the 'Yorkshire Dales'. You will find the same type of thing all over the North Riding, though none of it so very near the capital city.

Drive through DANBY ('Dan's Village', since 'by' is the Norse for 'village') where they play quoits with the same inimical friendliness as darts is played all over London. Go by FRYUP and POVERTY HILL with their views of purple moorland and emerald fields jigsawed with walls and hedges; ESKDALE, LANGLEYDALE, and GLAISDALE.

On a clear day the slightest movement may be detected in the valleys. A tree swaying, a pig sighing. Take the road over EGTON MOOR in a series of terrific climbs and enormous drops to the main WHITBY MOOR pass where hundreds of crows leap ungracefully about like London stockbrokers on the Floor of the House. And drive on through AILSABY to WHITBY itself.

The Abbey of Whitby, thrusting majestically upwards from the cliff, is the pride of the North Riding. The best view is from

154

the oddly-named KHYBER PASS. King Oswy of Northumbria gave land and tithes to St Hilda, the Abbess of Hartlepool, to found this monastery on the East Cliff. One of its lay members was the cowherd Caedmon, whose inspiration surmounted his illiteracy and who became father of the English sacred song. A synod was held here in 664 which consolidated Christianity in Britain and also settled the date of Easter.

And Captain Cook served his apprenticeship in a house in Grape Lane, now an antique shop.

Whitby, once a great whaling station, is the first point seen by the seaman on his return to land, the last he sees on leaving. It is large, clean, and full of character. The big harbour is flush with fishing and sailing vessels, the promenade curls attractively into the hillside. The ROYAL HOTEL is probably the most luxurious in the North Riding and faces the deliciously Victorian Spa Pavilion. From the hills around Whitby still come the polished jet beads so admired by Queen Victoria, though few craftsmen can now be found to hone them to the required brilliance.

From here you may visit SCARBOROUGH—which is large and modern—and ROBIN HOOD'S BAY, which is small, ancient, and full of history. Robin Hood's Bay is a book in itself and the best one has lately been written by Barry Farnille. It should be available in local libraries and should be read before visiting the village.

When you're not thinking about Captain Cook hereabouts you should certainly be thinking about Robin Hood. Morris calls him an 'eponymous hero' but the Dictionary of National Biography resolves him to the stature of a 'mythical forest elf'. Fordun, in the 14th century, mentions him in passing as 'that most famous cut-throat'. But certainly, whatever he was, BARNSDALE figures in every child's mind about him.

Robin Hood's Bay is, however, better known as a famous smugglers' haunt. The crowded buildings are said to be due to the reluctance of young married couples to leave their in-laws but nowadays I think they are probably also due to an extraordinary edict of Dr, now Lord, Beeching whereby it now takes two hours by train to reach civilisation, whereas it only took one hour before.

On the way back to Middlesbrough, through FYLINGDALES,

you might be lucky enough to find a Hound Trail in progress. These are announced in the 'Whitby Gazette' but it still isn't easy to find the actual location since it is always right in the middle of deserted moorland. I was lucky enough to discover the cheerful Captain Estill at the Shell FYLINGDALES FILLING STATION (Robin Hood's Bay 291) who made a telephone call for me to the next village in order to discover the exact spot on which this interesting manifestation was taking place. Possibly it might be best to ring Captain Estill to ask the way to his filling station before trying to find any Hound Trail on your own.

Hound Trails are not for the myopic. For a start you have to be able to spot a group of enthusiasts sitting right in the middle of nowhere, protected against possible heavy rainstorms in caps, sweaters, and gum-boots. After that you have to be able to pick out a tiny fleck in the middle distance running the wrong way, so that you are able to exclaim with the best of them: "Oh my gracious. Bert Lammas's Golden Rover has turned round!" Otherwise it is likely you may get rather bored.

The sport of Hound Trailing runs roughly thus: A couple of godlike youths rush away to a distance of approximately 7 miles dragging in their wake an old blanket steeped in a strong mixture of cod-liver-oil and old fox rotted in water. This is what is known in polite circles as 'The Drag'.

These godlike youths then rush back half an hour later pulling the old blanket athwart a gaggle of tethered Fell Hounds. (Note the Fell Hounds by now panting with excitement while the youths—having just run 7 miles at a hell of a lick—don't even look hot. Pause for admiring youths.) Every owner then lets his Hound loose and off they go, following the scent to nowhere. After about 15 minutes of freezing almost to death, a lot of little white specks appear on the horizon and everybody starts to whistle and yell and eventually the winning Hound yelps his way to his master to receive a pat on the head, a bucket of bran, and a short rest while he puzzles out why in God's name he had to run 7 miles to earn them.

From Fylingdales make your way along the coast to LYTHE, calling at the Red Lion for beer and fresh sandwiches which you'll need if you've been to a Hound Trail, thence to RUNSWICK BAY.

Runswick Bay includes HOB HOLE, once the abode of one 'Hob Thrush', a spirit invoked for the cure of whooping-cough. The Yorkshire man worries a lot about the fact that his coast keeps eroding and falling into the North Sea so it's as well to have a look at Runswick while it's still there. From here you can see KETTLENESS POINT where live the 'Yorkshire Bogies' who wash their linen in the Claymore Well.

And now to delightful STAITHES with its fisher-bonneted women and its little Portofino-type harbour edging deep into the cliffside. Here at lunchtime Mum and Dad may sit in the COD & LOBSTER watching their offspring rooting around on the beach and Mrs Hackett at the TULIP CAFÉ makes her own fresh bread and charges only 7/- for an enormous mixed grill. The cottages cling to the hillside right down to the very edge of the harbour, seagulls scream their heads off, and last time they had fireworks here somebody set light to the lot and the Fire Brigade forgot to bring any water. But it didn't matter. As the ice-cream man told me, it made a lovely 'conflageration' and he made a lot of money.

Captain Cook was apprenticed here before he went to Whitby, stole a shilling from his master's till, and ran away to sea. But that, according to Morris, was before he became respectable and started 'circumnavigating'.

Return to Middlesbrough by way of GRINKLE PARK, a really lush hotel at LOFTUS just outside the city yet slap in the middle of marvellous copper-beech and rhododendron. Unbelievable that this place with its deep coal-fires, ingle-nooks, large comfortable bar, huge garden, and fresh flowers everywhere is within two miles of a steelworks. A 3-course lunch is only 10/6d, bed and breakfast £2. And, as the brochure tells us, the Conservatory is only 'one fragrant feature'.

About twelve miles from Middlesbrough is SALTBURN. The SHIP INN here was once a smugglers' pub. One famous smuggling family, the Andrews, not only engaged in the contraband trade but were also Masters of the Cleveland Hunt.

Mr Hugh Cook, who wrote the little booklet displayed in the Ship Inn, tells us he still remembers when 'the whole of the coast from Coatham to Robin Hood's Bay was a hotbed of smugglers and legend tells us that even now large hoards of spirit and other treasure are hidden in the cliffs and rocks . . .'

I don't know though. I can't say I can see Jim Thompson

leaving large hoards of spirit *still* hidden in the cliffs and rocks . . .

Stephenson Clarke run some little coasters carrying coal all the way from Newcastle to Battersea to keep London going. I live near Battersea so, when the calls from my family, friends, and creditors finally began to verge on the querulous I asked Stephenson Clarke if they would take me back to Chelsea by sea?

"Good golly, no!" they cried, appalled. "You're a *woman*!"

Nice of them to have noticed. But . . .

Dear North-East Coast, I love you. And so that's all I *can* hold in my heart against you. Can't fish from North Shields, can't quietly drink in a pub on my own, can't go down a proper mine, and now can't go home by sea. All because I'm a woman.

Ah well. Come to think of it—you didn't ever force me to stand on a crowded bus either . . .